RACING
CREW

GW00357227

RACING CREW

Malcolm McKeag
and
Bill Edgerton

fernhurst BOOKS

Copyright © Fernhurst Books 1995

Second edition published in 1995 by Fernhurst Books, Duke's Path, High Street, Arundel, West Sussex, BN18 9AJ, UK

Printed and bound in Great Britain

All rights reserved. No part of this publication may be reproduced, stored in a retrieval system or transmitted in any form or any means electronic, mechanical, photocopying, recording or otherwise, without the prior permission of the publisher.

British Library Cataloguing in Publication Data:
A catalogue record for this book is available from the British Library.

ISBN 1 898660-16-6

Acknowledgments
The publisher and authors would like to thank Sunsail for the loan of a Sun Fast 36, and the following for crewing her during the photo sessions: Andy Beadsworth of North Sails, plus Mark Sheffield, Tim Powell, and Glen Kessels. Thanks also to Hunter Boats Ltd for the loan of an HB31 and Sue Fielden, Ewan McEwan and Paul Whitlock for crewing her.

Cover photo by Barry Pickthall/PPL
Photo on page 8 by KOS. All other photos by Chris Davies and Tim Hore

Edited by Jeremy Evans
DTP by Creative Byte, Bournemouth
Cover design by Simon Balley
Printed and bound by Ebenezer Baylis & Son, Worcester
Text set in 10PT Rockwell Light

Contents

INTRODUCTION

Offshore racing yachts come in all shapes and sizes from around 22 feet (7 metres) overall to 80ft (25m) on deck. The big boats – those over, say, 45ft (14m)– rarely take novice crews, for by a time an owner graduates to a boat of that size he has usually gathered around him a nucleus of crew who have been with him for several boats. In the rare instance of an owner starting his racing career with such a boat, the designer, builder and sailmaker will usually ensure that an experienced crew is found.

The majority of offshore racing yachts are under 40ft (12m) and in this fleet good crews are scarce. If you don't believe that, just watch an average class of 33 footers approaching a downwind mark in a smart breeze. The leaders will drop their spinnakers cleanly and round neatly, but towards the back of the fleet the sail-handling becomes more and more messy, until sooner or later comes the drama that gives the photographers their hairy pictures.

So this book is intended to help crew members – especially new crew members – who find themselves on that size of boat and want to know why the slick crews can change sails without anyone noticing, while *our* sail changes seem to take four people on the foredeck half-an-hour – and that's without anything going wrong; or why *their* spinnakers blossom forth at the windward mark like flowers in summer while *we* are lucky to get ours up with time for a beer before it has to come down again.

Malcolm McKeag and Bill Edgerton

1 It's Not Like Dinghy Sailing

The basic difference between big boats and dinghies is their size – much of this book is concerned with stating the obvious, but it is only obvious when you stop to think about it. In a two-man dinghy the sailors have to divide the work between them: the helmsman not only steers, but also trims the mainsail, hauls the spinnaker halyard, and adjusts the vang (sometimes called the kicking strap). The crew not only holds the jibsheet, but watches the opposition, helps with or calls the tactics, times the start, sets the spinnaker and often takes the blame.

Crew sizes

On a big boat there will be a number of people to split these tasks between. A 22-footer (6-7m) will usually sail with four crew, a 27-footer (8m+) with five, and a 33-footer (10m+) with six or seven. A 40-footer (12m), about the biggest we are likely to deal with here, will have nine or ten crew. A 50-footer (15m+) will have thirteen or fourteen, and the biggest racers, the 70 to 80-footers (21-25m), between twenty and twenty-four crew! The crew members will then have more specifically defined tasks, and need not concern themselves too greatly with others: indeed the bowman is well advised to keep his tactical opinions to himself, lest 'That Lot Back Aft' find something to complain about during his next spinnaker peel.

That does not mean the boat should be sailed by two people plus a gang of unthinking automatons: the best boats are sailed by a cohesive team where everyone thinks about the race and where very few direct orders have to be given, because everyone instinctively knows what to do. It does mean, however, that it is best to master the mechanics of big-boat sailing before trying to take over the management. If you are that good, your advice will be sought soon enough.

Bigger racing yachts will have at least 10 crew. Success is all about working as a team when the time comes for you to make your contribution.

Sail handling

The bigger boat's size also requires a completely new approach to handling sails. Even on a 27-footer, the spinnaker will be powerful enough to lift a man off the deck, so guile as well as brute strength is required to handle the sails. The principle tool in this is the winch (see Chapter 3), which is used to handle just about every piece of line on a big boat. On smaller yachts, some lines such as the main outhaul will be on multipart tackles, but the winch is still paramount. The new big-boat crew soon learns that his or her own strength is puny in comparison with the strength of the boat, and a new respect quickly dawns for the power of the wind in a sail.

Time off

Another major difference between dinghy sailing and big-boat sailing is the sporadic nature of the crewing job. In a dinghy, crewing is a continuing process, even if only leaning out, moving in, leaning out. In a big boat there are long periods where the sailing of the boat requires the immediate attention of only three or four of the crew: helmsman, tactician, main trimmer and genoa trimmer. The remainder of the crew sit where their weight does most good, usually on the weather rail with their feet over the side. Then comes a manoeuvre as simple as tacking or as complex as a gybe and spinnaker set, when a multitude of jobs have to be done in the shortest possible time.

Longer races

Not all races for offshore yachts are held offshore, but even a round-the-cans race for big boats normally lasts longer than a dinghy race. Twenty miles (1 nautical mile = 2,000 yards = 1.853km) is a normal race

for a small offshore boat, a short race for a big one - but even at six knots that is just over three hours, and if the breeze fails you might be out there for twice that time or more. Offshore races tend to be between 60 and 200 miles and may involve two nights at sea.

This extra time at sea means many things. Since the weather is seldom constant for more than a few hours, sails must be changed to suit the changing conditions. It is necessary to eat on board, and to sleep. Eating, sleeping and staying warm and dry are much more important on a big boat than in a dinghy. Most of us can put up with an hour or two's discomfort during a dinghy race, but becoming cold and wet at the start of a thirty-hour race is not only very unpleasant, but also reduces your own efficiency, and if things get really bad may distract the attention of other crew members who have to look after you.

Foredeck work is skilled and demanding, but is still dependant on total support from the crew in the cockpit.

2 Rules and Regulations

Although rules and regulations governing the race are primarily the concern of 'That Lot Back Aft' – the owner, skipper and navigator – there are some which directly concern the way the yacht is crewed during the race.

Handicapping systems

Virtually all offshore racing is done under some form of handicap system, even if within the handicap divisions there are separate prizes for yachts of the same design. The purpose of handicapping is to allow yachts of differing size and shape to race together and to allow comparison of their race times on some sort of common basis. Strictly speaking, handicap is the wrong word (the yachts do not have to carry extra weight, like horses in a horse race) and what we are talking about is a time allowance system. The slower the yacht, the more time allowance she receives for any race of given duration.

•Elapsed time and corrected time

The handicapping system applies a mathematical calculation to the actual time the yacht takes to complete the course, to convert it into the handicap time. To distinguish the two, the time the yacht actually takes for the race (measured from the time the race started – irrespective of when she actually crossed the start line – to the moment she crossed the finish line) is called the elapsed time. The time that is derived after the handicapping calculation has been done is called the corrected time.

It is the corrected times which are compared to find the winner of the race – the yacht with the lowest corrected time wins. Apart from establishing record times for a particular course – for example the Fastnet, Bermuda or Sydney-Hobart race – elapsed times are of no great interest in offshore handicap racing, it being in the nature of things that big boats go faster than little ones, which is why we have handicapping in the first place.

•Performance systems

The simplest systems are those which use observed performance information about the yachts to compare their results. If yacht A on average always completes the course 10 per cent faster than yacht B, then by adding 10 per cent to her elapsed time for a given day, and comparing it to yacht B's time for the same course on the same day, we can tell if on that day she sailed better or worse than yacht B. Few performance handicap systems are quite that crude, but it can be seen that the more times a yacht's performance has been observed the easier it is to fit her into the system.

Performance handicapping systems are often used for local club racing, but their principal disadvantages are that (a) they tend not to cope well with unknown yachts, and (b) it is difficult to avoid handicapping the crew, as well as the yacht. Who is to say how much of yacht A's

Unless you are in a one-design fleet, racing is staged against the clock as well as against other boats. The winner is decided on handicap, and everyone has an equal chance including the smallest boat in the race.

10 per cent advantage is due to her size and shape, and how much to the fact that she is better sailed than yacht B?

• **Measurement systems**

To overcome these disadvantages, measurement systems were invented. A measurement system tries to analyse mathematically the size and shape of differing yachts and somehow predict their potential speed. The yacht is then given what is called a TMF *(Time Multiplying Factor)* which is applied to her elapsed time to give her corrected time.

Depending on the complexity of the system, this might be just one number used for all races, or a whole series of numbers presented in the form of a complex table, the number-for-the-day being chosen depending on wind strength and even direction.

In the early 1990s a system called IMS *(International Measurement System)* was adopted for much top-level racing. In IMS, the yacht's measurements are run through a computer in what is called a Velocity Predicition Program (VPP). The VPP gives an entire profile of what the yacht's potential speed is in any wind strength and sailing in any direction. It also gives the TMF table. It hardly seems neccessary to add that a computer is also required to work out the result of the race – a concept that does not always have, shall we say, universal popular appeal. Much club-level racing thus occurs under systems not quite so complex.

Happily from our point of view, handicapping systems are of relatively low priority in the pit or on the foredeck. Our job is to ensure that the yacht is not handicapped – in any sense of the word – by her crew.

The rules and you

The handicapping system does affect us in one way, however. So that the yacht always remains in the same trim as she was when first measured, the rules are very strict about what may or may not be moved around on board while racing. Some items may not be moved at all: some items must always be kept in designated stowage areas (which must be clearly marked inside the yacht) unless the item is in use; and some items may be kept where you please, but must only be moved around if they are actually in use. Among the items which may not be moved at all are:

• The fuel and water tanks.
• The batteries.
• Any ballast which the yacht carries.
• The engine (even if you have a big enough spanner).

Items which must be kept in their marked stowage position unless actually in use include:

• The anchor.
• The chain.
• The spinnaker pole, if normally stowed on deck forward of the mast.
• The sails in their bags.
• The outboard engine.

Virtually every other item carried on board must be kept in its usual stowage unless actually being put to use. This includes crewbags, the toolbox, crates of beer, portable water containers and the liferaft. In particular, although the crew may move from side to side as the yacht tacks, they are not allowed to move anything else across the boat to act as extra ballast. To do so is to cheat.

Sitting out

The rules also prohibit crew members – apart from in exceptional circumstances – sitting or working outside the lifelines or guardlines. For the purpose of this rule arms, feet and legs are disregarded – hence the practice of sitting with legs and feet over the side – and on a yacht fitted with more than one guardrail, your head may be outside the top rail. As yachts have become lighter for their length over recent years, sitting out has become ever more important on offshore yachts, despite the patent absurdity of having a yacht with a cabin and beds which can only be kept sailing at its fastest with the crew perched on its extreme edge like seagulls on a harbour wall.

Watch a video of the best crews racing. See how during the tack those not actually pulling strings move across the yacht together, quickly slip themselves onto the rail and actually lean outboard together, often swinging legs, arms and torsos as far out as they can reach. If the top boys put that much effort into crew weight, you better believe it makes a difference.

3 Basic Hardware and Skills

WINCH LORE

It is sometimes said of modern racing yachts - as a criticism, not as a compliment - that the easiest way to immobilise them is to throw all the winch handles overboard. Unhappily (from a safety point of view) there is a great deal of truth in the criticism, but it points up the importance of the winch to just about every crewing task on board.

The end of the line - be it sheet, guy or halyard - which comes off the winch is known as the tail: hauling on this is called tailing, and the crew whose job it is is called the tailer. By keeping a load both on the working end of the line (in other words, the pull of the sail) and on the tail, the turns on the winch are kept tight and friction stops the turns slipping round the barrel or drum of the winch. A toothed ratchet inside the drum prevents the drum itself from turning. If, even pulling hard on the tail, the pull of the sail causes the turns to slip, one or two extra turns will give the line more grip on the winch and allow the line to be held.

Thus the winch allows the crew to hold (snub) a heavy load, or by turning the winch drum with the handle, to haul in a much greater load than even the strongest man could budge. Using the deceptive simplicity of the sheet winch, a woman weighing 100lb can easily control a spinnaker exerting enough pull to haul a 10-ton yacht.

Mechanical advantage

The mechanical advantage which gives winches their power is provided either by the handle alone or by combining the power of the handle with gearing in the winch. Modern racing yachts over about 28ft (8.5m) usually have winches that incorporate gears, giving two or even three speeds and thus doubling or tripling the mechanical advantage: on a big winch the power ratio available might be as much as 65:1. Such is the power of the modern winch; and such is the need, therefore, to avoid dropping the winch handles over the side.

Single-speed winches

The simplest form of winch. A toothed wheel (ratchet) inside the winch working against spring-loaded teeth (pawls) allows the barrel to turn one way but not the other. Most modern winches turn clockwise, but changing the ratchet will reverse the working direction of the winch: this is sometimes done for a particular reason or specialist application. Some single-speed winches have a second ratchet on the top, to allow the handle to be turned back, freewheeling, to give a more convenient pull. These are called single-speed ratchet winches.

Two-speed winches

On a two-speed winch, turning the handle one way - normally clockwise - turns the

Winches with two or three speeds are normal. The grinder should aim to wind at a steady cadence, changing gear as soon as the strain on the line threatens to slow him down. The tailer backs him up throughout the operation, and is watching the sail to give the word when he can stop winding.

drum at the same rate as the handle. Turning the handle the other way turns the drum more slowly, due to gearing inside the winch, and gives more mechanical advantage - just how much more depends on the gear ratios.

Three-speed winches

Extra gearing inside the winch allows either direct winding - like a single-speed winch - or one of two lower gears to be used. The gears can be selected with a button on the top of the winch and are so arranged that turning the handle one way (normally clockwise) gives direct gear, reversing direction gives second gear, and reversing direction again gives third gear. On most three-speed winches the gear-changing sequence, once begun, is automatic so the button has to be set only once - at the beginning of the tack, for example. The advantage of multi-speed winches is not just in the greater power they give but also in the greater control

they give when fine-trimming the sails, in particular the genoa.

Handles

Without the handle, the most powerful winch can be used only to snub a line that is to be held - it cannot be used to haul in the line. Handles are also expensive! So never leave a handle unattended in the winch: a stray line may catch it and flick the handle into the water, or cause some other foul-up.

The handle has a 'plug' at one end, at right angles to the arm, which fits into a hole on the top of the winch: some are square in cross-section, some star-shape. A square-head handle will work in a star-shape hole, but not vice-versa.

• *Simple handle*
This just has the square or star head, and is merely a lever to turn the winch drum.

• *Locking handle*
This has a small, turnable plate on the bottom of the star head which mates with a groove in the bottom of the hole on the winch head, locking the handle in position. The locking plate is turned by a little thumb lever on the top of the arm of the handle.

• *Double-handle*
This has two hand grips, set vertically above each other, and allows two people (four hands) to work the winch together. When working with a mate, work from the opposite side of the winch so that push-and-pull are combined: it is much more powerful than working side-by-side.

Coffee-grinders

These are the most powerful yacht winches, used mainly on yachts over 50ft

(15m). The handles, worked by two or four people, are mounted amidships on a central pedestal and turned vertically, like bicycle pedals. Gears and foot-switches are used to connect the grinders to whichever winch drum needs to be turned.

Self-tailing winches

Often used for halyards, control lines and runner tails on fractional-rig boats, as well as for sheet winches on cruising boats, the self-tailer has a device on the top consisting of a metal guide bar and a wide groove round the top of the winch. The tail is turned on the drum in the usual way and then led over the guide and into the groove, where it is held by friction and a series of ridges. As its name suggests, the self-tailer allows one person to operate the winch on his own, using both hands for the handle while the tail is automatically fed into - and out of - the groove in the top.

Cross-winching

Usually, the starboard sheet winch is used for the starboard sheet and the port winch for the port sheet, but if designer and builder have sited the winches to permit it, the starboard sheet can be led across the boat to the port winch, and vice versa. This is very useful on small boats where the last place we want the crew to sit on the beat is down to leeward. With cross-winching all the crew can be up to weather and the genoa sheet can be tended constantly without anyone having to move off the weather deck.

Riding turns

Normally, the turns on the winch lie one below the other, the line coming on at the lowest turn, round and round the winch and coming off to the tail from the uppermost turn. Occasionally, a lower turn traps over an upper turn - the cause is either a bad lead to the winch, or the winch turning too fast for the speed at which line is being pulled off, allowing the turns on the winch to go slack. When this happens, the result is a riding turn (or turns) and the line on the winch locks up solid and cannot be taken off at the top. Worse, the turns on the winch cannot be slackened to allow the line to be paid out. If the line is a genoa sheet, this means that the yacht cannot be tacked until the riding turn is freed, or the sheet cut.

The only way to free a riding turn is take the load off the working end of the line, allowing the turns to be freed from the bottom up. On a small sail it might be possible to do this by hand, but usually it is necessary to rig another sheet - the change sheet will usually be handiest. Attach this either to the sail at the clew, or to the working sheet using a rolling hitch. Lead the spare sheet through a conveniently sited block, or rig one quickly using a snap-shackle block or a snatch block. Finally take the change sheet to a spare winch (the spinnaker winch on the same side, or across the boat to another winch) and take the load. Once the weight is off the working sheet, the slack thus gained can be worked back through the turns on the winch until the jam-up is reached and the turn under the riding turn pulled free. Mind your fingers.

WINCH TECHNIQUE

Golden Rule Number One is always use a winch. The dinghy sailor or small keelboat sailor going aboard a bigger racing boat for the first time might be tempted to take a halyard or sheet in hand, especially - with a staysail for example - if the sail it is attached to looks small and innocent when on deck, or if the weather is light. One brief puff of wind, the sail fills unexpectedly, and nastily rope-burned hands are the result. Always use a winch.

Loading the winch

Ensure that the lead of the line to the winch is correct and that the line does not snag anything - the top of the cockpit coaming for example - or that it has not been led the wrong side of a stanchion. The line should rise to the winch at a shallow angle, so that it lands on the sloping shoulders at the lower end of the drum. If the line comes to the winch horizontally or, worse, at a slight downwards angle, riding turns will inevitably result: there must be no tendency for the line to ride up over turns already on the drum.

The winch will only turn one way, usually clockwise: if in any doubt, give the winch a spin before putting on the turns, then put the turns on the same way the winch spins. Just how many turns are needed depends on what is to be done: a heavy job will need more turns than a light job, but three turns usually give enough grip for most jobs, without having so much line on the winch that fast-hauling becomes difficult. The more turns there are, the more difficult it becomes to haul the line off quickly, and the more likely is a riding turn.

Extra turns

Often - when tacking, for example - it is best to have only two or maybe three turns for the light part of the job, then put on an extra turn when the real weight comes on. This is best done with the handle - which may have been used to wind in the sheet so far gathered - removed. The important things are to keep the weight on the line on the winch, so that the turns already on do not slip, and to ensure that your fingers are never on the inside of the extra turn where they could be trapped.

Keep the pull on the tail with the left hand, far enough from the winch to allow

the whole new turn to go on without having to move your left hand on the rope. Reverse the grip of the right hand. Now use the right hand to push the line onto the winch, moving the line round the winch at the same time. When your hand is on the opposite side of the winch, twist your wrist slightly to allow the line to go on the winch without your hand or fingers bring on the inside. By now all the load is taken by the right hand, always pulling the line onto the winch. Throughout, the fingers of the right hand - the hand nearest the winch - have been on the outside of the line as it goes onto the winch.

Trimming on the winch

With a powerful winch it is possible for just one person to wind in the sheet of an already set sail so smoothly that minute adjustments to sheet tension can be made. (If this is not so, the boat is under-winched - but as a recently joined member of the crew, forbear from mentioning it to the owner at this stage.)

To ease the sheet, tail with the left hand and use the palm of the right hand flat against the turns on the drum; first to press the turns against the drum as you ease the weight off the tail, then to ease the turns round the drum so the sheet eases gently.

First take a turn round the winch. Depending on the amount of load expected you should take one, two or sometimes three turns before pulling in. The more turns you take, the more chance there is of a riding turn if you pull in fast. As soon as the load comes on and you are unable to keep pulling in the line, put on enough turns to fill the winch barrel, slap in the handle, and start winding. On a small boat the genoa can often be pulled in most of the way without winding during a tack, and you can do the whole winching operation singlehanded. Once you have finished, always take the handle out and put it in its pocket. Left in the winch it is vulnerable to being lifted by a line and thrown over the side. You should then cleat or hand-hold the line, depending on preference.

You can ease the line on the winch with precise control using the method shown, even if there is a very high loading at the other end.

This way, you have precise control over how much sheet is eased rather than just letting the thing go, when it will hold on the winch and then suddenly jerk out several inches.

BLOCKS

The other principal item which the crew uses all the time is the block - what the layman and the ironmonger call a pulley. Blocks are used for a galaxy of tasks on board: rigged together they provide a tackle to give mechanical advantage (the most obvious example being the mainsheet); used singly they alter the run of a line either to avoid chafe or to give a fair lead. The position of some blocks is fixed, but most are movable and some blocks are positioned only temporarily, for a specific task.

Lead blocks

A lead block is any block whose job it is to give a lead to a line, either round a corner or, for example, onto a winch. Lead blocks may be permanently positioned, secured to the toe rail or deck eye with a shackle; or movable, secured usually with a snap shackle on a swivel.

The most obvious movable lead blocks are the sheet leads. These are usually mounted on metal sliders (sometimes with roller bearings and called cars) to run on tracks. They can be moved either by hand (fixed in position by a plunger which fits into a hole in the track), or by lines led through fixed blocks at each end of the track and thence to a winch or via a tackle to a jamming-cleat. Spinnaker sheet and guy lead blocks, for example, are moved freely up and down the toe rail or between pad eyes to give the required trim to the sail.

Snatch blocks

A very versatile block is the snatch block. This block is hinged at its swivel end to allow one of the cheeks (sides) to open, permitting the block to be fitted onto a fixed line rather than having to feed the line through the block in the usual manner. This is a very useful facility, and the snatch block is greatly used in spinnaker work, especially on larger boats.

Handy-billy

A handy-billy is just two blocks and a length of line, rove together to make a simple tackle, usually with a 2:1 purchase. The blocks have shackles, preferably snap shackles, to allow them to be clipped to suitable eyes, hooks or whatever. One of the blocks, the one that has the running end of the line, ideally has a cam cleat attached. The handy-billy can be rigged as a quick purchase to take a temporary load, hooked to the main boom and toe rail to prevent the main gybing, or used as a temporary sheet to free a riding turn - in fact for a hundred and one quick jobs about the boat. It is a very seamanlike tool to have available.

STOPPERS

Winches have two disadvantages: they are expensive, and they add weight. To save the latter more and more racing yachts are being built with fewer and fewer winches. In the 1970s a new 35ft (10m) yacht might have a dozen winches of assorted sizes, each dedicated to a single task. In the 1990s a 35ft racing yacht might have as few as four winches, requiring each to be capable of what in computers is called multi-tasking. The device that makes this possible is the stopper, a lever-operated gate through which the line passes on its way to the winch. Once the line is tensioned, the lever is dropped, jamming the line hard. The tail can then be taken off, freeing the winch for another task.

Stoppers come in all sizes. Different models work in slightly different ways, especially in how they are released. Some have a button which must be depressed before the lever arm can be released; with others you just lift the lever and shove it forwards or lift the lever and pull it back. The simplest way to find out is to check when there is no pressure on you or the line rather than halfway through a spinnaker peel. If the stopper is one you have not seen before, or have not used recently, for goodness sake ask a regular on board to remind you how it works. Any passing embarrassment will be as nothing compared to the emotions generated within your breast, and the breasts of those around you, if you wait til mid-manoeuvre then cannot get the wretched thing open. (Try "Any special tricks needed with the stoppers?" if you think "Just show me how these work, please" is too gauche an approach for a macho man like you; my own experience is that it is always better to act the innocent and then surprise them with how good you are, rather than the other way round.)

CLIPS

Lines such as the spinnaker sheets and guys and the spinnaker halyards usually end in some form of quick release clip. The simplest has a plunger with a piece of ribbon or line attached which, when pulled, opens the clip. A slightly swisher version has a latch which must be pressed downwards - often this too has a little ribbon tail to be pulled. With the plunger type you have to pull outwards at right angles to the clip; with the latch type you must pull downwards, along the line of the sheet, guy or halyard.

A common type, especially on bigger boats, has a large circular hole in the inboard base-plate in which is a trigger: squeezing the trigger releases the clip.

These are designed to be used with a spike which is rammed into the hole and jerked to fire the trigger. With the clip loaded-up the pressure needed on the trigger is considerable: unless you have fingers made of high-quality tensile steel do not be tempted to use your fingers instead of the spike.

MARKER PEN

Perhaps one of the most important items - so important you should always carry your own. Joining a new yacht you should find that almost everything, from runner tails to tracks for the jib-sheet cars, is blessed with a series of marks to indicate settings for various sails and various wind strengths. The secret of fast crewing is repeatability and precision - so instead of aimlessly pulling on a sheet or a runner tail until someone says "Stop", or it just won't come in any more, the sheet or tail carries a mark, and the crew know (and the newcomer quickly learns) that such-and-such a control is set with the mark so many

inches this side or the other of the winch or stopper. Every time you sail the boat, a better setting may present itself and the mark may have to be shifted, or just simply renewed. As your crewing skills improve and increase you stop going on boats as the newcomer and start making guest appearances. You may be able to suggest alternative settings, and when they result in more speed your personal marker will immortalise them.

Eventually, you will find yourself back on the sort of boat you used to sail on, before you were a really good crew - but this time you are there only after much persuasive pleading on their part, not yours.   This sort of boat never has anything marked. You wonder now how anybody can sail without little black ticks and lines all over the boat: it is literally like sailing blind. And when you show them the simple secret of marking, they will know you for the race-hardened expert you are and you will never have to buy your own drink again.

Stoppers are one of the most important developments in racing in recent years. They cut down on the number of winches needed on a boat, which in turn cuts a substantial amount of weight and cost. In the photos here, one winch controls four lines which are locked by stoppers. The 'up' position frees the line; the 'down' position locks it, but it can still be wound in.

4 Hoisting and Changing Headsails

Changing headsails is the fundamental crewing task on the modern cruiser-racer. Headsails have to be changed for a variety of reasons: a change in the wind strength requires a bigger or smaller sail; a change of course requires a different sort of headsail (from the heavy number one we used on the beat, say, to the jib-top we will use on the ensuing close reach); or even a change in the sea state - coming out from the lee of the land, the waves become bigger but the breeze does not increase and the skipper may decide on a fuller headsail to give more speed and power to cope with the seas.

In an effort to keep down the cost of racing, many one-design offshore racers limit the number of sails which may be carried: so many headsails, so many spinnakers and so on. Organising clubs also have similar rules and so too do many measurement and handicap systems, but there are still quite a number to choose from.

Sail stowage

Before the race all these headsails will be dragged from their usual marina-stowage and laid in their bags on the sole of the saloon, on the lower berths, and if the boat is big enough down beside the quarter berths too. On a well-organised boat (over a season it is the well-organised boats that do most of the winning) there is a carefully thought-out stowage plan. At the least, there is a list of all the sails on board posted prominently on the bulkhead, detailing the sail, what bag or sausage it is in, what wind strengths it can be carried in and where it is stowed while racing. The very best system is the one which uses big, clear labels actually over the place where the sail is lying. So, on the port-side inner slope of the coachroof you may find a large legend in black marker pen proclaiming:

> HEAVY NUMBER ONE
> NUMBER THREE
> HALF OUNCE
> JIB TOP

Where each sail is kept depends on the size of boat and number of sails: but in general the sails most often used should be easiest to reach, the heaviest sails should be in the middle, and sails adjacent in size or in order of use should not be stowed beside each other, to reduce the chance of the wrong sail being grabbed in a panic. Many jibs now contain battens: make sure you place these where they will not be stood upon and damaged.

HOISTING THE HEADSAIL

So now we have the sail on deck. Let us assume we have not yet started, and this is our first sail-set on board this yacht. Most racing sails are now kept in some sort of long flat bag or sausage. The major sailmakers have their own ideas about what is a good system, but in general the sail will

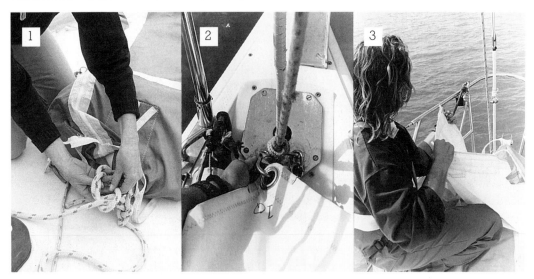

Attach the sheets with bowlines, keeping the loops as tight to the cringle as possible with a minimum amount of tail. Then attach the tack of the sail, which is usually slipped round a hook at the base of the forestay. Then check down the luff to make sure there are no twists in the sail.

be in a sausage which has a full-length zip. Ideally, this will be a fly-away zip and the sail can be folded so that the clew ring is at one end of the sausage, the luff with its head and tack rings at the other. With such a zip it is possible to bend on the sheets

The use of the luff groove is universal on racing yachts. Old fashioned hanks are in many ways simpler, but do not give the same aerodynamic performance and besides are heavy.

and attach the tack before undoing the zip; with the zip partly open, the halyard can be bent on, the luff tape fed into the feeder ring and up into the groove, and the whole sail kept secure and tight in the sausage until the moment to hoist. Then the zip is opened, the sausage skin peels away from the sail, and up she goes (and if the sausage skin has not been tied to something, it goes over the side). It is vital to check that the sausage can open right up before bending on the sheet. Some sailmakers do not favour the system just described, and fit closed-end zips. With these, the clew ring must be brought out of the zipper before the sheet is bent on.

Hanks and grooves

There are two ways in which the luff of the headsail may be attached to the forestay: by hanks or in a luff groove. For normal inshore and offshore racing a headfoil with luff grooves is almost universally used, but hanks are used on some older classes.

Clip on the halyard in the final seconds before the hoist and feed the top of the luff through the feeder and into the groove. Check aloft to make sure the halyard will run free.

The faster it goes up the better. Sweating on the halyard as it comes out of the mast speeds up the process. Everyone concerned in the hoist should watch the sail as it goes up to make sure there are no jams.

Most cruiser-racers and racers have three fore halyards. (Older yachts, especially if masthead rigged, might have four - two wire jib halyards, two rope spinaker halyards.)

Let us assume that our yacht has a headfoil (with two side-by-side luff grooves), two tack hooks and three halyards. An older yacht may have one headsail halyard (wire, emerging from the mast just below the forestay attachment) and two spinnaker halyards (rope, emerging just above the forestay attachment). Latest rope technology has given us halyards of Kevlar or Dynema (both registered trade names) with the flexibility of rope and more than the strength of wire, without the brittleness, while more recent mast design puts all the halyards above the forestay.

On very rare occasions it will be possible to predict what the next change will be and which tack the yacht will be on when we make it, and this rarity might influence our choice of halyard and groove. But normally we will begin on the middle or headsail halyard, with the tack on the port hook and the sail in the port groove. This way, the first sail change can be accomplished while on starboard tack, which is the tack helmsmen feel happier on if told they won't be able to tack for a moment because we are busy.

Feeding the sail

Having attached the sheets to the clew, attach the tack of the sail to the tack hook. Next follow along the luff tape with thumb and forefinger to make sure the sail is not twisted: this is very important, and if it becomes a matter of unvaried habit with every sail you handle, you will never have the embarrassment of that ultimate cry of foredeck failure: "Hold it - bring it down again!".

Having made sure the sail is not twisted, feed the head of the luff tape through the D-ring feeder, into the groove and attach the halyard. *Golden Rule Number Two: Never attach a halyard without checking aloft to see the halyard runs clear*

from the sheave to the sail. (At this stage all the other halyards will probably be clipped to their stowage hooks at the mast at deck level.)

At last the sail is ready to hoist. On very big boats the foredeck hand stays up forward to see the sail aloft and the mast hand hauls on the halyard at the mast, while the tailer winds the halyard winch. On smaller boats the foredeck hand does the mast as well. The halyard hand and tailer must watch the sail, in case of a jam at the feeder. Spot it now and it is easy to clear. Just keep blindly heaving and you really do jam it, or rip the luff tape of the sail, or both.

CHANGING THE HEADSAIL

There are three normal ways of changing the headsail: the bare-headed change, the side-by-side change and the tack change.

Bare-headed change

The bare-headed change is the least complicated, the least slick but not necessarily the slowest. The new sail is made ready, the old sail dropped, and the halyard changed to the new sail which is then hoisted. Of course there is a brief

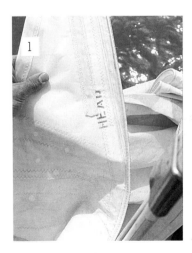

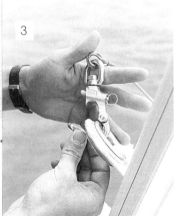

moment when the yacht sails bare-headed (without her headsail - hence the name) and thus rather slowly, but do not dismiss this method from the crewing repertoire. There are times when it is no slower and often quicker than struggling with a fancy change that has gone wrong. At night, in the rain, when it's blowing, with one wet sail sticking to the other and two people on the foredeck struggling and exhausting themselves, only to find the halyards have been crossed, the crew boss might well wish he'd called a bare-headed change and had the yacht going again ten minutes earlier. Another time when the bare-headed change is frequently best of all is in very light, ghosting weather. With the yacht just creeping along, minimal disturbance and crew movement is paramount and she will lose very little with a bare-headed change done quickly and gently.

Side-by-side change

In a side-by-side change the new sail goes up alongside the old sail, inside or outside depending on which halyard is in use. The yacht stays on the same tack throughout and the old sail comes down alongside the new sail. The problem is either hoisting the new sail, or lowering the old sail, or both. Which side the new sail goes up depends on which halyard is already holding up the current sail. If the old sail is on the middle or starboard halyard, and the yacht is on starboard tack, the new sail will have to use the port halyard (middle if available) and groove and thus be fed out under the old sail, dragged aloft between it and the guardrail and sheeted home. Then the old sail can be dropped inside the belly of the new sail - this is an outside hoist/inside drop.

With an inside hoist/outside drop the reverse procedure is used. In either case a new sheet, called the change sheet, must be rove and bent on to the new sail: usually it will be rove through the spare car, placed in the correct sheeting position for the new sail. With a capful of wind in the sails, and especially if the sails are wet, the

Outside Hoist/Inside Drop: (1) The new sail goes into the headfoil outside the existing sail. (2) Pass the new halyard forward, making sure it is outside everything and free to run before (3) clipping on to the head of the sail. (4) At the same time the sheets should be bent on, with the bag secured on deck. (5) When everything is ready, hoist the new sail. (6) Then pull the old sail down.

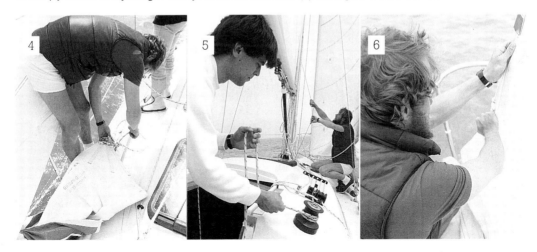

Tack Change: The new sail is hoisted inside the existing headsail which is the easy way to hoist. As soon as it is up, the yacht tacks. Mid-tack, the halyard of the old sail is let go while the new sail is sheeted in. The foredeck hands pulls down the old sail on the inside, which is the easy way to drop.

drag caused by skin friction between the two can be enormous and even two people tugging on the luff tape will not be enough to budge the wretched thing. The conversation then runs (to the person on the winch):

"I pray you, friend - let the jolly halyard go."

"With all my heart I assure you, friend, I have let the halyard go this long time - pray pull a little harder..."

One trick is to lift the skirt of the inside sail, if that is the one to come down, to let air up between the two to effect separation, or the old clew can be brought forward to achieve the same end. A quick luff by the helmsman can help here. This sticking problem can be really troublesome, and much time can be lost with the yacht plugging along with her bows and her speed well down.

Tack change

The tack change alleviates the problem wholly. The yacht is tacked when the two sails are up and the old sail is fluttered down on deck as she comes through the eye of the wind. This is a fast and slick method, but requires good timing. Things must be arranged so that the yacht is on the opposite tack to whichever halyard is set. Let us suppose she is on port tack with the set sail on the middle halyard and in the starboard groove. (If it is in the port groove with the starboard halyard use a bare-headed change - who wants a crossed halyard?) The new sail goes up inside the set sail on the port halyard and in the port groove. There is no need here to use a change sheet, for the lazy, weather sheet is unbent from the set sail and bent to the new sail from what is still the weather side. With the sail aloft and the new halyard made, the yacht is tacked and the new sail sheeted home with the port-side sheet, the sheet of the old sail having been let go in the normal manner.

As she comes through the eye of the wind the old halyard is let go and a quick tug on the luff brings the sail on deck with a will - and neatly inside the new sail. This method gives the best of both worlds: inside hoist and inside drop.

Final thoughts

With every sail change, remember to check that the sheet lead is right for the new sail, especially if the reason for the change is a turn in the course. The number three blade does not usually set too well when sheeted to the same place as the jib top.

Times can arise when you are faced with the choice of doing a bare-headed change or intentionally crossing halyards. Suppose we are reaching on port with the number two genoa up on the genny halyard, port track, with the reaching spinnaker on the starboard spinnaker halyard. The next leg is a beat, and we will want the number three genoa - it will either have to go up in the starboard groove but on the port spinnaker halyard, or the 'two' must be brought down and the 'three' sent up the starboard groove on the genny halyard.

On some boats the spinnaker halyards come out of the mast far enough above the headstay fitting for it to be safe to lead the halyard over the top - but now you must make sure that when the spinnaker comes down, it comes down to starboard of the mast and forestay. If the next mark is starboard-hand and the skipper for some reason decides to gybe the chute and then drop - the foredeck team are in big trouble. There has to be a very good reason for allowing halyards to cross intentionally. Most of us have enough trouble with the unintentional crosses we have to bear.

Once the old sail is down, the halyard is clipped either to the pulpit or back to the mast and the slack taken up straight away, before the loose, swinging halyard has a chance to hook round a spreader or to jump the sheave and jam at the masthead. Get the weight off the foredeck quickly by bringing the sail aft, along the weather deck if on the wind. Usually there will be time to bag the sail on deck before sending it below - stowed back in its proper place, not just dumped at the companion steps. Often it may be felt that the change is only temporary and the sail just taken off may be the next one needed. Here the sail can be kept on deck, still tacked-down and lashed with sail-ties to the guard-rail or toe rail. Do not leave a sail thus all night, especially in conditions with spray on deck - bag it and send it below.

Finally, tidy up. Check the position of all the halyards, and their safe stowage. Check that the weather sheeting position has been

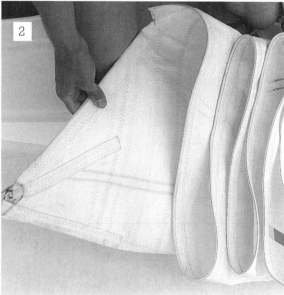

altered to match the leeward one - and that the new weather sheet has been bent to the new sail. Check its lead (has the sheet crept under the spinnaker pole, or been passed inside the babystay?) so you are

sure the yacht is clear to tack. "Just a minute" is not too helpful a reply to the order to tack with the yacht hurtling towards the shallows.

SAILS YOU MAY MEET

Headsails
(attached to forestay)
Drifter
No 1 genoa
No 2 genoa
No 3 genoa
No 4 genoa (sometimes called 'working jib')
Jib top (high-clewed reaching sail)

Staysails
(smaller sails used in front of mast, but set flying)

Mainsail

Spinnakers
0.5 oz (called the 'half-ounce')
0.6 oz (often called the 'thirty-twenty', from the type of cloth)
Reacher
Runner
Storm spinnaker (sometimes called, for obvious if rather unfair reasons, the 'chicken chute').

Bagging a Sail on Deck: (1)The sail is pulled out along the side deck, and (2) flaked along the luff and leech with the tack protruding and (3)a sail tie securing the forward end. (4) The bag is put over the sail upside down, then the whole lot is flipped. (5) If the two sides of the zip are staggered with the slide pulled past the join, the bag can be pulled open without unzipping.

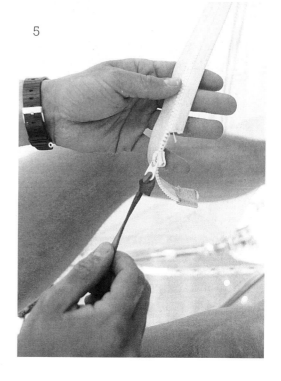

5 CHANGING TACKS

Look at a video of good match racing, or a top competition like the Champagne Mumm Admiral's Cup, and watch the top crews tack the top yachts. From fully powered-up with her crew out on the rail the yacht glides into the turn, swings through the wind's eye, heels and settles on the new tack with her crew somehow out on that rail, the speed hardly seeming to falter. You simply don't notice what goes on in between.

Watch a mid-fleet yacht in a club evening race do a tack. Assuming there is anyone on the rail to begin with, you will see them come off and take up their positions. You will hear the skipper bellow "Lee-ho", hear the bang and see the shape-change as the genny eases, then stops, then backfills as the yacht heads up into wind. You will then see it catch up on the weather shroud as the yacht continues her turn, drag across the front of the mast then flog out past the leeward shroud, be half-wound in and stop. You will then see the extra help go down to the winch, hear the skipper urge "Come on - wind it, wind it...", see the keelroot and much of the rudder of the yacht break surface as she heels, see and hear - but need we go on? It's as painful to describe as it is to watch.

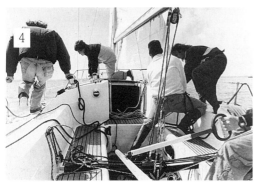

A bad tack, like the one above, can cost a yacht fifteen seconds - and that's without anything going 'wrong' - against a flawless tack. In a race with twenty tacks, that is five minutes. Most yacht races are won or lost by a margin of less than five minutes.

TACKING TASKS

As with every other manoeuvre, we need to decide in advance who will do what. Here are the jobs, from aft forward:

• Runners
• Helm
• Mainsail
• Headsail
• Ballast

It is simply not worth ascribing priorities or degrees of importance, because each on its own is entirely capable of at best screwing-up what might have

been a nice tack, or at worst costing quite a bit of money.

In general the sequence of events is:

1.   The new runner is made ready.
2.   As the helm goes down the new runner is pulled on, the old jibsheet is flung off, the weight-watchers come in off the rail.
3.   As the yacht comes upright the old runner is flung off and the new runner is wound on, the old sheet helped out, the jib helped round the mast, the slack taken up on the new jibsheet and the weight-watchers move across.
4.   As the yacht pays off the new jibsheet is pulled in, the main traveller and sheet eased, the weight-watchers get on the rail and get their weight as far outboard as humanly possible to help the yacht power up.

Smooth tacking. In the moments before the tack a crewman moves smartly across the boat to tend the leeward winch. Two other crewmen come off the weather rail to take their positions at the windward winch. The sheet is thrown off the leeward winch, as the boat comes round and the new leeward sheet is pulled in. Note how the first crewman moves smartly to the new weather rail as soon as his job is done. Meanwhile, the other two crewmen grind in the last part of the sheet. One stays down to leeward to trim, while the other gets up on the weather rail. It's taken less than half a minute.

It is important to know exactly who does what and who goes where during a tack. If necessary someone must be ready to help the genoa round the front of the mast.

5. As the speed rebuilds, the jib is trimmed on and set, the main traveller brought up and the sheet trimmed on.

Runners

You may well find this is the first job you are given to do when you join a new yacht. Considering how much a new mast costs, and how just one mistake with the runners can ripple or kink the mast - or even drop it over the side or the bow - such a job allocation represents something of an act of faith on the crew boss's part. The important thing is to understand what the runners do. They hold the mast up.

The runners will usually have their own winches. As the tack is called, overhaul (pull on) the slack from the leeward runner until the runner itself kisses the leeward belly of the mainsail. Do not over-tighten the lee runner at this stage, or you upset the shape of the main. If the forestay has an electronic load guage, check the numbers for setting up the new runner on the new tack.

Take the tail of the windward runner in hand, ready to get it off the winch. As the yacht comes upright, pull on the new runner, the tail of which should have a black ring-marker round it which gives a

setting for how hard the runner is wound-on. Your first time doing this, you will usually be told where the mark should finish. Once the yacht is through the wind's eye, cast off the old runner and make sure it can run. It must not get in the way of the mainsail or boom as they fill on the new tack.

Once the old runner is off, set the new runner to its appropriate setting using the load guage, or the black mark on the runner tail. Tidy up the old runner, overhauling the slack, ready for the next tack. Short tacking, the old runner is just left swinging, but on longer legs it is taken forward to the shrouds to keep it from chafing the back of the mainsail. NEVER, EVER secure the tail of the lee runner. If the yacht has to bear away quickly, the boom can be held in by the secured lee runner: the sail will not go out, the mainsail overpowers the rudder which stalls out and the boat rounds-up into the wind. If the original reason for the bear-away was to dip the stern of a right-of-way yacht coming across, rounding-up is probably not what the helmsman wants to do.

Slick speed is the essence: the runners must be set and un-set smoothly, without shock-unloading the mast. You do not have

much time before the rig loads-up again on the new tack, but in fact the danger of dropping or damaging the rig during a tack by mishandling the runners is slight in all but the heaviest weather, since the standing rigging (forestay and shrouds) and the mainsail will hold the mast in safety. Gybing is rather different, and is dealt with later in this book.

Mainsheet

Leaving the helm to the helmsman, the mainsail can both help the yacht into her tack, and power her out of it. On the slickest-crewed yachts, the main traveller comes up as the helm goes down, helping turn the yacht. Traveller and sheet should both be eased, the sheet by as much as two feet (60cm), the traveller to halfway below whatever will be its setting once the yacht is up to full speed. If the main is not eased, it fills as soon as the yacht is through the winds' eye, before the yacht is properly moving on her new tack and before the waterflow over the keel has properly re-established itself - before the keel has grip, in simple terms. It then just blows the yacht over on her side, she slides sideways, the rudder stalls out and the speed comes tumbling down.

The main trimmer must watch the speedo. No yacht should drop more than two knots at any stage of a tack - on a good tack the speed loss can be as little as half-a-knot. Most of the speed loss during a bad tack is down to the mainsail trim: if something goes wrong with the jib, the helmsman can drive off using the main and keep the speed up, or even tack back - but only if the main trimmer is really on the ball.

Headsail

Before the tack, have the new genoa sheet loaded on the new winch - three turns - and the handle ready to drop in. As the yacht goes into her tack, hold the old genny sheet until the genny luff starts to lift - then 'blow' the sheet. Blowing something off a winch is a deliciously descriptive term for what you have to do. We are not talking just letting go of it: we are talking dumping the load, flicking the tail and the remaining turns off the winch and making sure the line runs out fast and free, all in one smooth flowing movement. Like everything else aboard a yacht, it is worth practising.

As the yacht rises, the foredeck hand, who should be the forwardmost person on the rail, gets up, swings monkey-like around the front of the mast and catches the genny, helping the sail around the mast and the new leeward shrouds so there is no foul-up. While this is happening, the new leeward sheet is overhauled fast on the winch, and hauled in until the sheet loads up. One more turn is spun on the winch, the tailer lays back on the tail, and the winch-winder drops the handle into the slot and starts to wind. With the sail more or less home the trimmer takes over the tail and begins to set the fine trim on the genoa while the tailer gets up and out on the rail.

Trimming the yacht

Everybody else trims the yacht - this includes even important people like the tactician. The group of weightwatchers come off the rail as they feel the yacht come upright going into the tack. Those not assigned specific tasks slide across the yacht as she rolls through the tack, and get themselves on to the rail just as quickly as they can. It can hardly be overdone, for the more weight on her rail as the wind begins to press against her sails on the new tack,

the more power the yacht has at her disposal to drive herself forward, out of the tack.

A good crew establishes a routine about who sits where on the rail, so each can take their place quickly. By keeping the same places, each can work out with the others the quickest route across the yacht, and use it every time. This way there are no traffic jams: the fluidity should be akin to a well-drilled rugby football pack forming a scrummage (imagine the shambles if every time a scrummage formed, its members took different positions - sometimes in the front row, sometimes the second, some-times on the flank - depending on their fancy and the order in which they arrived as the scrum was called down). Remember that you are not on the rail because you have no job to do: your job is vital, no less than keeping the yacht on her feet.

Letting off the old sheet and sheeting in on the new side is a matter of synchronisation and communication between the crew and the helmsman who can help their task by feeding the boat through the wind. The sail should be virtually sheeted in before it fills on the new tack.

Sometimes the foot of the genoa sticks on the guardrail as it comes in. Giving the rail a bang with your hand at the critical moment will normally unsnag it. With the tack complete, the trimmer brings in the last few inches of sheet slowly to help the yacht power up.

6 Trimming for Windward Speed

On a well-sailed dinghy the crew continually move their weight to compensate for gusts and lulls. Not only does this prevent the boat capsizing: she will sail faster and can be steered more easily if the crew react smartly to changes in the wind's strength.

The yacht sailing beside her has a ballast keel to prevent a capsize, so the need to react to changes in the wind is less apparent. It is perfectly possible to trim her sails, cleat the sheets and sail to windward with only the helm being tended. The only problem is that if the yacht is sailed like this she will seldom win races; to do that her crew will need to trim the sails constantly and carefully - they are, after all, responding to the same changes in wind speed that keep the dinghy crew in continual motion.

On a yacht with a masthead rig the governing sail upwind is the genoa: it is much bigger than the mainsail and is working ahead of it, so it takes the wind first before passing it back to the mainsail. On a yacht with a fractional rig the main is more important, although the headsail, being ahead, still has a profound effect on the trimming of the main.

On short inshore races it is relatively easy to give sail trim the attention it deserves: all the crew are on watch all the time, the best people stay on their allotted jobs all through the race, there are other yachts close by to out-sail throughout the race, and it will not be uncommon for an inexperienced crew member to complete the race without touching the main or genoa sheets.

On a longer race constant attention to sail trim becomes the task of every crew member, for it is on a long race that the temptation simply to cleat the sheets and sail along is greatest: there may be no

If you want to get to windward fast you have to trim. Don't just cleat off the sail controls and leave them until the next tack.

The headsail trimmer must watch the sail at all times. It's a tiring job, and on a long race the trimmer should be replaced periodically.

other yachts close by with which to compare speed, and what's a second or so in a day-and-a-half race? Look at it this way: in a 36-hour race with an average speed of 5 knots, an extra hundredth of a knot is worth over four minutes at the finish line. Even if we can't squeeze an extra 0.01 out of her, can we not make sure we don't drop a great deal more by failing to notice those slight changes in the breeze? Think of the dinghy sailor, constantly leaning out, leaning in, leaning out...

Communciation

A word about communication. While you're trimming you may find the helmsman using a cryptic code which the newcomer finds either confusing or just unintelligible. Most controls move up or down, in or out, or backwards or forwards. Many instructions call merely for 'on' and 'off': but the logic is very simple. Whatever movement of the control gives the yacht more power is 'on', and the opposite is 'off'. Thus 'Sheet on' is sheet in; 'Runner off' is runner tail eased, and so on.

Some calls require more than one control to be moved. 'Main off' usually means traveller down, but may also require the sheet to be eased as well; 'Main on' will usually mean traveller up (pulling the boom in) and mainsheet in (pulling the boom down).

THE GENOA TO WINDWARD

The trimming tools available on the genoa are:

*   The halyard
*   The sheet
*   The sheet lead position (both fore-and-aft and athwartships)
*   The backstay (or runners if fitted)

Coarse adjustment of the sheet is used to adjust the angle of the sail to the wind. Fine adjustment of the sheet and the halyard together are used to adjust the shape and fullness of the sail. Movement of the sheet lead position is used to adjust the amount of twist in the sail. Increasing backstay tension pulls the forestay tight (on a masthead rig) reducing luff sag.

All of these can be adjusted easily under load, except the sheet lead position. This is because the sheet pulls the slider upwards, making it impossible to move the lead block along the track. The trick is to pull that part of the sheet ahead of the block downwards, so the slider will move fore or aft along the track. On a smallish yacht this might be achieved just by pushing down on the sheet or by standing on it, perhaps easing the sheet slowly at the same time.

On a bigger yacht more elaborate techniques are needed. If standing on the sheet does no more than improve the view you get of the other yachts, clip a snatch block onto the sheet ahead of the lead block. Lead a line from it through a spare car further forward on the track (or through a spare lead block clipped to the toerail), and then to a winch. Wind in on that line - easing the sheet at the same time - and the sheet will be pulled down to horizontal, allowing the lead block to be moved. On longer races, the change sheet is often left bent-on, allowing quicker reaction to small changes in wind strength. On some boats this system is permanently rigged in lieu of (or in conjunction with) conventional tracks and sliders.

On the latest race boats, the jibsheet cars are of roller bearings, with either a block-and-tackle or a line led via a stopper to a winch, by which means the car can be pulled forward even under some load.

When doing so, ease the sheet to ease the adjusting of the car, even if you intend winding the sheet back on when the car is reset.

How to trim the genoa

The main aids to trimming (apart from our own two eyes) are:

* The telltales (every racing headsail should have three pairs positioned about 10 inches aft of the forestay at quarter, half and three-quarter height.
* The speedo.
* The panels of the sail itself (or better still, trim tapes - those thin black ribbons across the sail seen on the classier racers).

1. Set up the genoa depth (belly curve) by eye for today's conditions (the trim tapes will help here).
2. Adjust the runner tension to set up the forestay tension, and thus the entry angle of the genoa. (On a masthead yacht pull the backstay fairly tight. This in turn pulls the headfoil tight, taking much sag and round out of the luff of the genoa.)
3. In smooth water and with a good breeze for the sail, trim for pointing ability. Reduce the fullness of the sail by tightening the halyard, but not so much that a crease appears in the form of a hard line down the luff. Tighten the sheet, but avoid pulling the sail taut around the base of the shrouds. The front part of the sail is now fairly flat, allowing the yacht to point high although she is critical to steer, there being only a narrow `groove' in which she is going fast.
4. In a shifting breeze, or in waves where more power is needed (even at the expense of pointing) it may pay to ease halyard, sheet and runner or backstay a

The spreader ends are an important indicator as to how far to wind in the genoa. The sail should never be tight against them.

little. This gives the genoa more round (the depth of the sail increases and the point of maximum draft moves forwards). The helmsman will find the boat less critical to steer on the wind, i.e. there is a broader `groove'.

Using the telltales

Next use the telltales to check you've got it right. Your objective is to provide the helmsman with three pairs of beautifully streaming telltales which all break together as the boat luffs. To get the telltales streaming ask the helmsman to hold the boat on the wind:

* If the windward telltales will not stream the sail is trimmed out too far. Check the helmsman isn't pinching, then wind in the sheet until the telltales stream.
* If the leeward telltales will not stream

The object is to provide the helmsman with beautifully streaming telltales which all break together as the boat luffs

An easy way to discover what each control does is to over-adjust each in turn and watch the effect. Over-tightening the halyard produces a hard line down the luff, over-easing results in wrinkles at the luff and the horizontal trimming stripe shows the effect on fullness.

the sail is too close. Check the helmsman isn't off the wind, then ease the sheet until the telltales behave. Next, ask the helmsman to luff slowly. All the windward or all the leeward telltales should move together.

- If the upper windward telltale misbehaves first, there is too much twist in the sail, cured either by tightening the halyard or moving the sheet lead forward.
- If the lower windward telltale misbehaves while the upper telltales stream correctly, there is not enough twist to the sail and the halyard must be eased or the sheet lead moved aft.

NOTE: It may be the yacht sails best not with all windward and leeward telltales streaming, but with the windward telltales just lifting - that's fine. The important thing is the telltales lift together. Telltales are visual aids, not blind rules.

Experiments with controls

A very easy way to discover what effect each control has on the sail is to over-adjust each one in turn while leaving the others fixed (this is best tried when not racing). Set the sail up, then deliberately over-tighten the halyard until the hard crease appears; now ease it and note what happens, not just to the luff but also to the head of the sail. See how it starts tight and flat, the leech curling back inboard and perhaps against the upper spreader end. Then as the halyard is eased fullness appears in the head of the sail, and the leech opens out until, with the halyard too soft, the leech at the head flutters, the luff becomes uncontrollable and the position of maximum draft moves aft until it is more than halfway between the luff and the leech.

Now do the same with the sheet lead, starting too far forward. See how the leech comes hard down from the headboard,

If the car on the headsail sheet lead track is too far forward, the foot will be too loose and the leech will be too tight as shown in the first and second photo. Move it too far back, and the opposite will happen. Get it just right, and the sail will be perfect as shown in the last photo.

while the foot of the sail is so rounded and baggy it bellies out against the guardrail; move it aft and watch the leech open; see how twist grows in the sail until with the lead too far aft the leech flutters, the head of the sail will not fill and the foot is pulled flat and tight. Watching the sail change shape will bring all the theory to life.

THE MAINSAIL TO WINDWARD

The mainsail is controlled by:
- The halyard
- The outhaul
- The sheet
- The traveller
- The vang
- The cunningham
- The flattener
- The backstay and runners

The mainsail, with a rigid spar along two of its three sides, is easier to control than the genoa. On a fractional-rig yacht it is also more important than the genoa.

Here again the trick of over-trimming each control in turn will illustrate dramatically the effect that each control has. To start, we assume for simplicity that the boat has no runners.

1. The halyard and the outhaul adjust the shape and fullness of the sail.
2. The mainsheet is used on the wind principally to control the amount of twist in the mainsail.
3. The traveller controls the angle of the boom - and hence the sail - to the centreline of the yacht.
4. On the wind the vang helps control the twist, and on yachts with powerful vangs and flexible booms it will be used to vary the depth of the sail at the bottom and near the mast.
5. The cunningham is merely an extension of the halyard's power. On virtually all yachts there is a maximum distance between the head of the mainsail and the bottom where the boom joins the mast (usually marked by black bands

The mainsail trimmer controls his sail with the traveller and mainsheet fine tune lines. These are led to the windward side of the cockpit, from where he can get a perfect view of the telltales near the leech of the main. In stronger winds the traveller is left down the track, and the trimmer trims with the mainsheet fine tune; in lighter winds the traveller is brought up the track, and the trimmer trims with both the traveller and mainsheet fine tune, holding one in each hand.

on light coloured masts, light bands on black masts) so the cunningham is needed to tighten the luff further when the sail is already at maximum height.

6. The backstay (on a fractional rig) controls mast bend and, therefore, fullness in the mainsail.

How to trim the mainsail

Sailing a fractional rigger upwind, the principal sail trimmer is most usually on the mainsail, using sheet and traveller in much the same way that the dinghy sailor's weight is used to keep the boat on her feet and moving freely.

Light and medium winds. The main aids to trimming are the telltales down the leech of the mainsail, ideally positioned one at each batten pocket. Your objective is to keep all the telltales streaming and have very little backwinding in the front of the main.

Firstly use the traveller and mainsheet to align the main boom down the centreline of the boat:

•   If all the telltales are streaming gradually increase mainsheet tension, at the same time letting the traveller

down to leeward so the boom stays on the centreline. You are reducing twist in the sail – continue to do this until the top telltale begins to curl in behind the sail.

•   If the top telltale(s) are misbehaving let off the mainsheet, at the same time pulling the traveller up to windward. The boom stays on the centreline and the sail twists until the telltales stream again.

Stronger winds. While the mainsheet controls mainsail shape, the traveller controls its angle of attack and is to the fractional-rig yacht what the accelerator pedal is to a motor car. If the yacht seems overpowered, ease the traveller down; if she is underpowered (most likely with dead or with lee helm), bring the traveller up until full power is restored. In gusty conditions the traveller will have to be dumped frequently, but if it spends more time dumped than putting on power, it is time to reef.

The main traveller has a profound effect on something other than just the mainsail: the rudder. As the power comes on and off the mainsail, the effect on feel and rudder balance is enormous. Here, the helmsman and trimmer must communicate continuously: on the best boats they use few words, for the trimmer can tell just by watching the wheel or tiller how much helm the yacht is needing, and apply power or ease it as required.

Runners

Runners are adjustable lines that run from the middle section of the mast down to the side deck near the stern. There may be one or more runners on each side of the boat. On a masthead-rig boat the runners simply control mast bend: increasing runner tension reduces mast bend and so increases the fullness in the mainsail. On a fractional rig the upper runners meet the mast near the hounds, so increasing runner tension tightens the headstay. If a set of lower runners (checkstays) are fitted they are used to control mast bend.

THE TRIMMING LOOP

Not what the youngest member of the crew is sent to fetch on a quiet day in the marina, but the process by which everything and everyone responds to everything and everyone else. The sails cannot be set and trimmed in isolation - each reacts with the other - and in a fractional boat the mast is so trimmable that it must be regarded as being almost as flexible as the sails. A re-trim of one element will require an adjustment of each of the others, while over-setting one will throw the others off balance also. Over tightening the leech of the genoa, for instance, will not only take too much twist out of that sail, it will throw the mainsail inside-out. Pulling on a runner will take draft out of the mainsail - but will also ease the leech of the headsail while flattening the entry. This may require correction via the genoa sheet.

Practice and observation

Nothing teaches trimming skills so much as constant practice coupled with analytical observation. A useful set of priorities for the beginner to work on getting right is to start with the jib luff, then the mainsail leech. When these are right, start work on the middle of each sail and the middle of the rig (the mast setting). When these are right, go back and check the front of the jib, then the back of the main. An endless loop of trim, trim, trim.

REEFING

All the crew become involved when it is time for the flattener or for a reef to go in. Slab reefing is now virtually universal, and systems are almost standard. The depth of the reef is dictated by the position of the reef cringles at luff and leech. Usually the luff cringle is fitted over a hook at the gooseneck, and the leech cringle pulled down by a line made fast at the boom end, rove through the cringle, down into or along the boom and brought out at the mast. It is then led down the mast and back to a winch.

Reefing procedure is simple, but if each step is not taken logically much sweat and even breakage can result. We need to tend the halyard, the reefing line, the vang, the mainsheet and the luff of the mainsail. Never begin reefing until each member of the team knows which controls he or she will attend.

When all is ready

1.   Ease the halyard (the immediate effect will be that the boom will drop markedly, which is probably why so many crews neglect to ease the sheet and vang later).
2.   Pull the luff down, fit the ring over the hook and take up on the halyard straight

away, to prevent the ring from falling off the hook again.

3.   Ease both the sheet and the vang. Then take up the slack on the reefing line, take turns on the winch and wind in the reef.

Note that it is imperative to ease both sheet and vang, otherwise the winch winder has to wind against these, effectively trimming the sail by the reef line alone. It is likely that the reef cringle will be pulled out of the leech of the sail, or the reefing line will break under the enormous load, or the mainsheet or vang fittings will start to pull out of the boom.

Some crews are reluctant to ease that mainsheet right away, thinking that by keeping some power in the mainsail through the reefing process they are losing less speed. The opposite is usually the truth: the sheet is eased right away, the sail flogs briefly, the reefing line is banged home and the sail re-trimmed within a few seconds.

HEADSAIL CLOSE REACHING

Yachts which go distance and passage racing, indeed any that race on other than a windward-leeward or triangle course, spend much time with the sheets just eased: not hard on the wind, but at the same time not far enough off to carry a spinnaker. This facet of racing is pure boatspeed and little else; but it can call for a fair amount of sail handling and plenty of crew work - much more than sailing hard on the wind.

In smooth water the helmsman should be steering as straight as a die while the trimmers adjust the sails not merely to the changes in wind strength but also to the wind direction, using the speedometer as the final adjudicator of their success. Just how straight a course is steered depends on how good the helmsman is and on the rapport between helmsman and trimmers: the hallowed dinghy technique of 'up in the lulls' and 'away in the puffs' does not work

Reefing: Reeve and tie off the reefing pennants beneath the boom if this has not already been done. Ease the halyard, hook in the reef tack cringle, and then re-tension the halyard. Ease both the vang (kicker) and mainsheet, and wind in on the reefing pennant until it's hard down on the boom. Finally re-tension the vang and mainsheet.

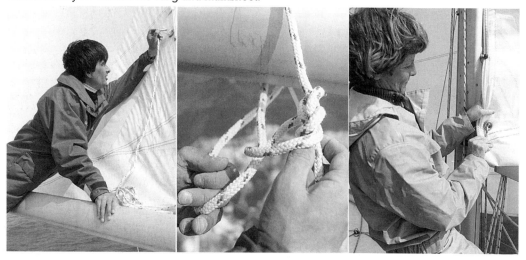

so well, if at all, on bigger yachts which do not plane.

On yachts up to 33ft (10m) the sails used will usually be simply the mainsail and number one genoa (probably the light number one if there is a choice, as it will usually have a higher clew and be fuller cut than the heavy); on bigger yachts there will probably be a specialised reaching jib - often called (quite wrongly but rather romantically, conjuring as it does memories of days when yachts set real topsails) the jib-top - and perhaps a staysail to set inside the jib-top.

Trimming the genoa

As the wind hauls aft and the sheets are eased we trim for speed, and the first rule of thumb is trim the genoa, then the mainsail. In two-sail reaching the slot between genoa and mainsail is every bit as important as in upwind sailing.

As the genoa sheet is eased the clew of the sail will rise, throwing more twist into the sail. More twist will be required anyway, to keep the slot open at the top once the mainsail is eased, but if there is too much twist the top of the sail will not fill

and drive when the bottom is right: and if the top is set right, the lower part of the sail will be over-trimmed, backwinding the main.

Here again the telltales are valuable. The genoa will work within a wider range of angles of attack than when on the wind, and it will be possible to ease the sheet and have the weather telltale lifting long before there is any suggestion of the luff back-filling. The rule of thumb here is to trim to the leeward telltale, and often the windward telltale will be lifting considerably.

As the wind hauls further aft - say to about 50 degrees apparent - the weather telltale can be ignored completely, for it will be hanging lifeless inside the sail where it curves away from the forestay. As long as the three leeward telltales are working together, the twist is about right. The leech of the genoa and the leech of the main should follow similar curves till they meet at the masthead, while on a fractional rig, the leech of the genoa should be following the curve of the mainsail's belly.

Barber hauler

As twist increases, the top of the sail will

Rounding up from a reach to a beating course. Notice the mainsheet is first pulled in using the 'coarse' end, then using the 'fine tune' end. Finally the traveller is adjusted as the trimmer studies the mainsail telltales.

stop working - the misbehaving telltale being the first sign. Now is the time to start moving the sheet lead position forward, to take out some of the twist. Unfortunately, moving the lead forward also tends to pull the clew of the sail inboard, just when we want it outboard (to open the slot and to leave room for the mainsail to be eased as well).

So we need a way of moving the lead position not merely forward but outboard and downwards as well. For this we use a barber-hauler: a snatch block clipped onto the sheet between the lead block and the clew. A line from the snatch block is led through another block clipped to the toe

The barber hauler is a useful device to pull the headsail sheet lead outboard and downwards.

rail or a pad-eye to a winch, and this is winched in as the sheet is eased. The effect is to pull the sheet out of line, and provided the toe-rail block is correctly positioned we can adjust the sheet and the barber-hauler until we have the clew of the sail just where we want it.

Runners and backstay

The other adjustment we need to make is to the runners or backstay. Ease them well off from the upwind setting to put more draft into the body of the sail.

Other reaching sails

By now it may be time for the jib-top, if the sail inventory includes one. This is set exactly like an ordinary headsail, using a full-height halyard and the luff groove on the headstay. Because of the high clew the sheet lead position will be well aft, but because the sail is specially designed for this point of sailing it will seldom be necessary to barber-haul it.

Staysails are seldom worth the effort on yachts under 30ft (9m), because what they add to the speed is often more than subtracted by the speed loss incurred through the disturbance of setting and trimming them; but on bigger yachts they

are used a good deal. `Staysail' is a complete misnomer - yet one more example of modern yacht usage taking an age-old seaman's word and turning it upside down - because the sail is not set on a stay at all but is set flying, inside the curve of the jib-top. Whereas the jib-top is cut with a high clew, the staysail is cut with a very low clew and its job is to increase the flow of air through the slot between the jib-top and the mainsail - in particular low down where air is `escaping' under the high-cut foot of the jib-top.

The yacht may have a staysail purely for use with the jib-top, or she may have a dual-purpose sail for this job and as spinnaker staysail. The reaching staysail has a shorter luff and foot: the dual-purpose staysail will have a full-height luff, but with extra cringles part of the way up the luff to act as the tack when reaching and at the leech to act as the clew.

The reaching staysail is tacked down to a deck fitting not quite halfway aft between the forestay and the mast: often the tack fitting is on a track, to allow adjustment. A single sheet is all that is required, led to a fairlead forward of and inboard of the jib-top sheet lead. If there is a staysail halyard, it will emerge from the mast at about two-thirds height, otherwise a spare masthead or spinnaker halyard or, if it is high enough, the pole topping lift, is used.

MAINSAIL CLOSE REACHING

With the genoa trimmed we turn our attention to the mainsail. Yet again, the telltales - this time off the leech of the sail - are our principal guide to how well the sail is working, while the tools at our disposal are the sheet, the traveller, the vang, the halyard and the outhaul.

If the true wind strength remains constant the apparent wind speed - the speed across the deck it is sometimes called - will drop as the yacht bears away onto a close reach. This, combined with the change of angle, will require all the mainsail controls to be reset. The halyard and the outhaul must be eased, the traveller let down to put the boom at the desired angle and the sheet eased to put more twist into the sail. The vang will probably need to be eased too.

Crew weight will have to be kept aft, more so than when beating, and on very wide-stern boats with the maximum beam far aft, it may already be time for one or two crew members to move their weight aft of the helmsman. You get a great view, perched on the aft quarter.

If the runners or backstay were not touched when trimming the genoa, look at them again now. Straighten the mast to put more draft into the mainsail, and if the boat has checkstays, ease them off.

7 Setting the Spinnaker

No sail provides a greater single test of a yacht's crew than the spinnaker. By watching how the spinnaker is set, trimmed, gybed and handed (`dropped' is a word we might care to avoid - too often it is only too accurate a description of what has happened), observers can most easily pick out the well-crewed yacht from the badly crewed yacht, and badly crewed yachts have to have big reserves of boatspeed or very good navigators if they are to win races regularly. By the same token, the crew member who can approach 'Spinnaker Time' with confidence and competence is worth half-a-dozen tactical experts as the gybe mark looms ahead.

Spinnaker handlers

Yet spinnaker work is like most other crewing tasks: it just needs common sense and logic. Its special ingredient, however, is teamwork. Only on the smallest boats can the spinnaker be handled completely by one person: on a 25-footer (7.5m) the team will usually be two, one doing the deck work and the halyard, the other tending the lines (topping lift and downhaul, sheet and guy) in the cockpit. On a 30-footer (9m) there might be four: one on the foredeck, one at the mast and two in the cockpit. Each member of the team must have his or her assigned tasks and responsibilities: unless the team has worked together often and recently, talk each

Confidence in spinnaker handling is one of the great keys to race winning.

manoeuvre - hoisting, gybing or whatever – through beforehand to make sure everyone is expecting the same thing to happen in the same order. One person doing the wrong thing at the wrong time can wreck an otherwise beautiful day.

SPINNAKER GEAR
Halyards

All but the simplest one-designs will have two spinnaker halyards, usually of aramid-core rope such as Spectra or Dyneema.

The spinnaker halyards always emerge from the mast above the point where the forestay joins the mast (even on a masthead-rigged boat) so that the spinnaker, when set, is free to swing across the front of the forestay, setting on the port or starboard side of the yacht as required, or being shifted across when gybing.

Unlike the mainsail or genoa halyard, the spinnaker halyard is not played as part of the sail controls: the spinnaker is either up, or it is not up. In all but the smallest boats, however, the halyard will nonetheless be taken to a winch. This is primarily to give control over the halyard when the time comes to lower the sail: in hoisting the spinnaker, the sail should be virtually at the masthead before there is any real weight on the halyard, other than the weight of the cloth, and good crews on even quite big boats can have the sail aloft by hand using the winch only for the final few feet of halyard.

From the left – lazy guy, spinnaker sheet, jib sheet over pole, guy, lazy sheet.

Topping lift and foreguy

The topping lift and the foreguy (on smaller boats sometimes called the downhaul, as it is on a dinghy) which support and control the spinnaker pole will also be led to winches. Even on a 22ft (6.5m) masthead rig yacht, the spinnaker is big enough to pull against a strong man unless the mechanical advantage of a winch is used. It is quite common now for the foreguy to be rigged so that it has two tails, one along each side of the deck.

POLE SYSTEMS

The spinnaker pole is the all-important element in controlling the spinnaker. The sail itself is probably the biggest sail on the boat, yet it is set in certainly the most

precarious manner. Therefore the pole must act as a rigid spar to hold the outer corner of the spinnaker, and to do this it must itself be rigid, and held firmly in place.

This is achieved by having the inboard end of the pole secured to the mast, the outboard end held firm by the triangulated support given by the topping lift (holding it up), the foreguy (holding it downwards and forwards) and the spinnaker guy itself, pulling it downwards and aft. The bigger the boat and the bigger the spinnaker, the bigger, stronger and more complex must be the pole and its rigging. On the largest yachts it may take three men to lift the pole, lock it onto its mast fitting and winch it aloft with the topping lift acting like the jib of a crane.

Double-ended pole

This is the simplest system, like that used in most dinghies, except that in yachts the pole is not stowed along the main boom but on the foredeck. The pole itself is light enough to be handled by one person and has identical fittings at either end. One end clips to the mast fitting, the guy runs through the other. Note that the spinnaker pole should never be attached directly to the sail.

To gybe the double-ended pole, the inboard end is unclipped from the mast, passed across the foredeck to the sheet and clipped to it. The outboard end is unclipped from the guy, the pole is pushed right across, and what was the outboard end now becomes the inboard end and is clipped to the mast.

Through all this, the pole is supported by the topping lift, and to keep the pole

balanced this support must be spread evenly along the length of the pole. This is achieved by having the topping lift come to the middle of a wire span or bridle which itself is secured to the two ends of the pole. The downhaul goes to the middle of a similar bridle, underneath the pole. (Topping lift and downhaul are not attached directly to the middle of the pole because the spinnaker itself acts on the end of the pole, and to attach the pole supports to the middle would cause it to bend and probably break).

With this system, only one line is needed to each corner of the spinnaker, acting as both sheet and guy. The lead from the deck will be varied, using a snatch block or a simple barber-hauler, depending on whether the line is acting as sheet or guy. This system is usually found on masthead-rig boats up to about 27ft

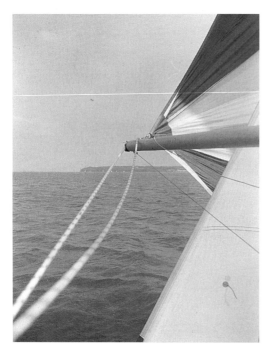 

Left: Correctly rigged - sheet over guy. Right: Incorrectly rigged - the lazy sheet under the pole results in problems when gybing.

(8m), but can be used on fractional-rig boats up to about 33ft (10m): it all depends on the size of the spinnaker.

Single-ended pole

When the size of the spinnaker requires a pole too heavy to be swung about the foredeck by one person, or when the sail is too big to be gybed dinghy-style, the safer but slower single-ended pole is used. The fittings are usually different at either end, with a plunger or latch-operated clip at the outboard end through which runs the guy, and a conical plug at the inboard end which fits into a cup on the mast. The cup on the mast is mounted on a slider which runs on a track on the fore side of the mast, allowing the height of the pole to be adjusted.

The type of pole fitted and the gybing technique used go hand in hand. With a single-ended pole, the so-called dip-pole gybe is used (see Chapter 8). For dip-pole gybing it is necessary to have two lines to each corner of the spinnaker, not one. We have a separate guy and sheet rigged on each side, and the line not in use is called the lazy guy or lazy sheet. For example, on port gybe, the pole will be on the port side and the sail trimmed with the port-side guy and the starboard-side sheet; the port-side sheet, although attached to the sail, is doing no work and is called the lazy sheet; the starboard-side guy is also doing no work, and is thus the lazy guy. On the other gybe, the port-side guy is the lazy guy, the starboard-side sheet the lazy sheet.

Having gone to the expense of duplicating the sheet and guy on each side, we can take advantage of their presence to refine the system. Usually, sheet and guy will be led differently (the guy being led further forward than the sheet), and

different types of rope can be used for each. The guy takes greater loads than the sheet and must not stretch, whereas a bit of stretch in the sheet is no bad thing. The guy will usually thus be heavier than the sheet, and may be of aramid core. It is always the sheet which is attached to the sail, the guy being attached to the end-fitting of the sheet, usually by a clip onto a stainless steel ring. This is to facilitate letting go the tack of the spinnaker when the time comes to hand the sail.

With a single-ended pole, the topping lift and foreguy can be taken direct to the outboard end of the pole. Indeed, the foreguy is normally left clipped on, and is used to secure the pole in the stowed position.

Dual system

Yachts of around 30-32ft (9-9.75m) often combine these two systems, using a double-ended pole with duplicated lines. This allows flexibility in crewing since the style of gybe (end-for-end or dip-pole) can be selected depending on the weather conditions.

HOISTING THE SPINNAKER

Remember the 'five peas': Proper Preparation Prevents Poor Performance. Make everything ready before the spinnaker is needed, then as little time as possible need be spent on the foredeck before the spinnaker is ready for hoisting.

To button-on the spinnaker, we need:

- The sail on deck, and the sail bag or turtle attached to something so that it will not blow overboard.
- The sheet and guys led correctly to the correct corners (clews) of the

spinnaker, and attached.
- The halyard attached to the head (not the clew) of the spinnaker.
- The pole clipped to the mast and set up on the topping lift with the guy led through the outboard end of the pole.
- *The Golden Rule is everything must be led outside everything else.*

The sail in the bag

The bag or turtle with the sail properly packed inside must be brought on deck to the place where the sail will be launched. On small boats this will be the pulpit or from the main hatch; on bigger boats the lee rail, under and outboard of the genoa. Use the tie-tapes on the underside of the turtle to tie it to something solid to prevent it blowing overboard when the sail is hauled out. Spinnaker turtles are not merely expensive, they are difficult to make during a race and you may need it again before the finish.

Sheets and guys

Lead the sheets and guys to the turtle. The windward pair, which will be the guy and lazy sheet, must go outboard of the windward shrouds, outboard and forward of the forestay and to the sail, coming over the top of the guardrail. The sheet and lazy guy come round the leeward rigging and over the top of the guardrail. Although the spinnaker will set as well inside-out as outside-out, most will have a green patch at one lower corner and a red patch at the other. The sail should have been packed with the green (starboard) patch to the right of the head and the red (port) patch to the left, so it makes good sense to follow the convention and position the turtle with the corners pointing the right way (green to what will be the starboard side when the sail is up, red to what will be the port side) and then clip the starboard lines to the green corner and the port lines to the red corner. All this lessens the chance of the sail going up with a twist in it.

Below: Hoisting the spinnaker with the clew hard against the pole. You can hoist away with the sheet almost on, pulling it tight as the head hits the top. Then drop the headsail.

It is always the sheet which clips to the sail. The guy clips to the ring set through the sheet clip, or to the clip itself. The reason for this is so that should you need to you can always take the guy off (if the wind falls light, for instance, or you want to do a peel – see Chapter 9) without letting go of the sail.

Halyard

It also means that the only corner left unattached to which the halyard can be clipped is the head, which is usually white. It is very embarrassing to hoist a spinnaker on its side with the halyard clipped to the clew, but some of the best crews in the world have done it - which shows that it is also very easy. If there is a choice, use the leeward spinnaker halyard, leading it outside the genoa and over the top guardrail to the sail. If the windward halyard must be used (after several sail changes, it may be that the headsail is on the leeward spinnaker halyard) make sure that it leads clear from the masthead over the forestay and down to the sail. Remember: everything outside everything else.

Setting the pole

Note that the pole is used with the end clips opening upwards. Unship the pole from its stowage, make sure that the downhaul (or foreguy) and the topping lift are tended and free to run. Clip on both. Put the inboard end to the mast fitting, with the outboard end lying on deck where it is free to lift without catching under the guardrails or pulpit, or under the genoa. The best place is lying to weather of the forestay, inside the pulpit legs.

The foredeck hand supports the outboard end of the pole while the weight is taken on the topping lift, partly raising the pole until it rests against the weather side of the forestay. Pause here to put the guy through the end fitting of the pole, making sure that the lazy sheet lies on top of the pole. This is very important. If the lazy sheet hangs under the pole, when the time comes to gybe the pole cannot drop down free from the guy but becomes caught between the guy and lazy sheet. This spells trouble in a big way, the most expensive version being where the pole ends up sticking out through the front of the spinnaker.

Top up the pole to the required height, and the foredeck department is ready to go.

Meanwhile, back aft

In the cockpit, things must be happening to support what is going on at the front of the boat. The sheet and guys must be tended, principally to see that the foredeck hand has enough slack, but also to see that there is not too much slack, with lines going over the side, round the rudder, propeller or even the keel. The topping lift and foreguy must be tended constantly, and when the pole is being set it is important to ensure that there is plenty of slack in the weather guy and sheet. If there is not, the corner of the sail will be pulled out of the turtle as the pole is raised, and will fill with wind and pull the rest of the sail out. This will happen behind the genoa and probably not be seen until the sail appears in a bundle in the water alongside the cockpit. Everybody will notice then.

The windward genoa sheet must be slack enough to allow the pole to be topped-up. If not, at best it puts a downward load on the pole and topping lift, and the first time you want to gybe the sudden antics of the pole become a

In this instance the halyard and guy are wound up and in almost together, with the sheet pulled in as the spinnaker goes up.

headache for the foredeck hand in more ways than one; at worst you will not be able to top the pole correctly at all.

Here we go

Everything is ready. Make sure that there is:

- Someone on the halyard, with back-up if needed.
- Someone on the sheet.
- Someone on the guy.
- They all know what is going to happen when the cat comes out of the bag, and what they have to do.

If necessary, the crew leader should talk through the operation with everyone, so that all know exactly what is happening, what they have to do and that nothing has been forgotten. The order to hoist should be given either by the skipper if on deck, or by the watch leader. Everyone must know beforehand whose voice will give the

signal, and that person must be very sure that the yacht is ready for her spinnaker. Do not forget to check with the helmsman - many is the spinnaker that has started its way aloft while the helmsman was still trying to shave past the mark. If the sail touches the mark the yacht must do her 360 degree turn to exonerate the fault, and all that slickness and preparation have been for naught.

Hit it!

The spinnaker in the bag is safe and easily controlled. The spinnaker filled with wind but firmly held at head, clew and tack is safe and easily controlled. Between these two states, the spinnaker is just trouble looking for somewhere to happen - so it stands to reason that the shorter the transitional stage, the better. *The Golden Rule is Get it Up, then Get it In.*

The tack of the sail should come out of

the bag first, followed by the head. Unless the set is something complicated, such as a gybe-set, the tack can be 'sneaked' - pulled out to the pole end just before the order to hoist is given. As the head rockets toward the mast the pole should be coming aft, to clear the sail from behind the genoa, let air in around the luff, and prevent the sail from twisting. Most twists which are not caused by bad packing are caused by letting the spinnaker wallow and flop in the turbulent air behind the headsail, where it eventually (indeed quite quickly) revolves around itself. Do not wait until the sail is up before hauling aft the guy. The clew can look after itself.

If the sail is launched in this manner, the clew will blow away to leeward as the tack (and with it the luff of the spinnaker) comes round the forestay and finds the wind. Then, when the sail is properly up and the halyard secure, the sheet can be taken in and trimmed and the sail will fill beautifully. If, however, the sheet is trimmed too soon,

the spinnaker is pulled into the windshadow of the genoa and mainsail where there is no wind to fill it. As the guy is, belatedly, hauled aft the clew drags across the back of the genoa, the foot tightens across the back of the genoa, and soon the genoa stops working as well. The boat slows right down, just when she should be accelerating. So:

- Guy first, sneaked to the pole end.
- Halyard next and fast.
- Pole aft quickly.
- Sheet in when it's up.
- Genoa halyard off to drop the head of the genoa and let air into the spinnaker.

Don't overwork the halyard grinder. The other problem with sheeting in too quickly is that the sail fills before the halyard is right up and secured. At best this means that the last few feet of halyard have to be ground in, which is just unnecessary hard work; at worst, the weight in the sail

The famous twist or 'hour glass'. The way to undo it is to pull on the luff; if that doesn't work, ease the halyard as well.

defeats the halyard grinder, the halyard runs back out and the sail falls in the water.

Headsail down

The most common mistake which follows a quick, neat spinnaker hoist is failure to get the headsail down quickly. Watch a video of the hot crews in action. See how the instant the spinnaker head hits the top, the genoa starts to slide down the forestay - even before the spinnaker sheet is drawn aft. The reason is to let air into the head of the spinnaker, to help the sail fill. There is a temptation to try to keep the genoa drawing and thus provide power until the spinnaker is drawing and can take over. Resist it. The most common cause of spinnakers taking a long time to fill is that the genoa is disturbing the air flow into the sail. It can even cause a well-hoisted spinnaker to go into a twist, while promptly

dropping the genoa has served to blow more than one twisted spinnaker clear. Do not worry too much about getting the genoa right off at this stage: it is the top of the sail causing the problem. So dump the genoa halyard, and let the sail fall part the way down the luff groove of its own accord. Do not wait until you have someone in the bows.

THE GYBE SET

We have described the conventional leeward set, with plenty of time to make ready and set the pole. Sometimes the race dictates we approach a windward mark on one tack, round it, gybe and go away on the opposite gybe. During this manoeuvre, the spinnaker has somehow to appear.

Everything is made ready as before, except with the spinnaker on what is still the windward side. However, we cannot set the pole up, because the genoa is in the way: but we can be very nearly ready.

Setting the pole

Clip the pole to the mast in the normal manner, but with the outboard end out under the genoa, using the foreguy to keep the pole end close to the forestay. The pole end must not drag in the water, or be allowed to slide down and out under the leeward guardrail. The topping lift is clipped on but left slack, making sure that it has been led under the genoa sheet. The inboard end of the pole is raised to the required height.

As the yacht bears away into the gybe, the genoa is eased out and quickly pulled across the pole. As soon as the genoa is across and the old genoa sheet let right off (to give the needed slack), the pole can be topped up in the normal way and the spinnaker set.

The hoist

Timing is the essential element of success. As the boat bears away into her gybe, the apparent wind drops dramatically. If you start hauling halyard as the boat comes upright, you should find the spinnaker up and setting before the wind catches up again. Very satisfactory. Everything in the cockpit works the same as for a bear-away set except the sides are reversed. Be careful not to pull the pole aft before it has been topped up, otherwise the end swings under the guardrail and the pole remains pinned on the foredeck. Much urgent conversation inevitably ensues.

8 Trimming the Spinnaker

A spinnaker is just a spinnaker, no matter how big the boat, so the rules for trimming it on a yacht are the same as on a dinghy. The difference lies in the size of the sail and the power it produces: the spinnaker on even a small yacht will produce more than enough power to pull a crewman off his feet and over the side. So the mechanics of big-boat spinnakers are more complex.

Turns on the winch

Both the sheet and the guy must be led to winches and the first *Golden Rule of spinnaker trimming is Never Take it Off the Winch.* The guy should always have at least two turns round the winch; while for the sheet, the number of turns will be whatever is needed to grip the sheet, so that there is no pull on the trimmer's arm with the sail full and drawing.

The trimmer gets the best view of the spinnaker from the weather deck. The number of turns needed on the winch depends on the pressure of wind, and how much winding needs to be done.

In very light weather there might be just one turn on the winch so that the sail can be given sheet each time it needs it, and in a breeze three turns may be needed. In ghosting conditions even one full turn may be too much on a small spinnaker; the sail will not draw the sheet out against even that small amount of friction. In such conditions (by which time lightweight light-weather sheets will have been rigged) take the turn off the winch but continue to lead the sheet from the turning block round the winch barrel to your hand. This way (apart from giving the correct lead) you still have the friction of a half-a-turn round the barrel of the winch to help cope with stray gusts and cat's-paws, and if the wind does pick up quickly a complete turn can be put on in a twinkling. Taking the sheet right off the winch, to lead straight to hand from the turning block, sooner or later results in rope-burned palms. Don't do it. On yachts over 30ft (9m), even the topping lift and foreguy must be worked on winches all the time.

Organisation

It is the size of the spinnaker, rather than the size of the yacht, which determines spinnaker organisation, but as a guide we can equate a 27ft (8m) masthead-rig yacht with a 33ft (10m) fractional. Above this size, trimming the spinnaker sheet is a two-person job. The trimmer has to hand the tail of the sheet, and stands or sits wherever he or she has the best view of the sail (some of the best spinnaker trimmers on smaller yachts - where brute strength is not needed - are women). The winder is positioned at the winch, with the task of cranking the winch every time the trimmer calls the sheet in. With enough weight in the sail for this to be required, a minimum of two turns will be needed just to stop the winch barrel slipping inside the turns of the sheet, but with more than three turns it will be difficult to get the sheet to run out sweetly to ease the sail.

BASIC TRIMMING RULES

Symmetrical spinnakers
- The spinnaker should be symmetrical about its own vertical midline.
- Unless the boat is being overpowered the spinnaker should be shaped and trimmed to present the maximum possible area (called the projected area) to the wind.
- The spinnaker pole should be at right angles to the direction of the apparent wind (the wind across the deck).

- The tack and clew of the sail must be at the same height off the deck; thus the foot of the sail is horizontal.
- The pole should be horizontal, or slightly cocked upwards at the outboard end. The pole should never point downwards from the mast.

Asymmetrical spinnakers

Trim an asymmetric as you would a reacher, adjusting the pole height to ensure the luff breaks evenly. Trim the sheet first, to fill the sail. Then set the luff properly. Then fine-trim the sheet. If the pole is too high, the spinnaker luff has too much curve, rolls too quickly and the whole sail sags off to leeward. If the pole is too low, the luff is too tight, the entry will be too fine and the sail will keep collapsing too easily. Once the luff is set, the sheet is eased until the luff folds at the same time down virtually its whole length - then trimmed a fraction to stop that happening.

The pole

Once the sail is up and drawing, the

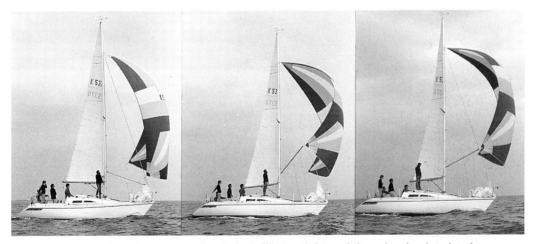

Left: Pole too low. The clews are not level, the luff is too tight, and the spinnaker is twisted to windward. Centre: Pole too high. The spinnaker is now twisted to leeward. Right: Pole almost right, but the inboard end should be raised to bring the pole more horizontal.

Left: Oversheeted - the spinnaker is too far round with the slot closed.
Right: With the sheet eased, the spinnaker pulls the boat forwards rather than sideways.

helmsman should steady the boat on the required course. With the boat on course, bring the pole aft (by winding in on the guy) until the luff of the spinnaker starts to collapse by folding in on itself. The guy should then be eased out, allowing the pole to go forward, by three or four inches - just enough to stop the luff curling. Remember that every time the guy is moved the foreguy (or downhaul), which is acting against it, must be tended also.

Keep watching how the luff comes off the pole end. It should be vertical, and with the luff tape aligned fore-and-aft. If the luff is leaning outboard, bring the pole aft. If the luff is leaning inboard, ease the pole forward. Glance regularly at the masthead wind indicator to check the pole is at right angles to the wind direction.

The sheet

With the pole and guy properly set, ease the sheet until once again the luff of the sail starts to fold in upon itself, then pull the sheet in about four inches until the luff stops folding. The sheet and guy are now correctly set.

Because the direction of the wind is never constant, the spinnaker sheet must be constantly on the move. Even if the true wind remained constant in direction and speed, the very act of trimming the spinnaker correctly affects boatspeed and thus apparent wind. Trim the spinnaker properly and the yacht immediately picks up speed. As she accelerates the apparent wind draws slightly ahead, requiring the sheet to be brought in. The boat reaches her maximum speed for that breeze and is no longer accelerating: the apparent wind draws aft again and the spinnaker is now over-trimmed. The boat starts to slow. All these minor changes in apparent wind direction can be dealt with by the spinnaker sheet, but it must constantly be on the move. *The Golden Rule of spinnaker trimming is Ease it.* For every properly trimmed spinnaker in the fleet, there are two which are over-sheeted. From a trimmer's viewpoint, it is a fact that the spinnaker is at its most efficient and fastest just on the moment of collapse. Constant

Left: With the pole too far forward, the luff and leech collapse together.
Right: With the pole too far back, the luff falls in and the foot is pulled tight across the forestay.

trimming is necessary to keep the sail just at that critical, but fastest, point.

Pole height - outboard end

The clew of the sail, to which the sheet is attached, if free to find its own height naturally, depending on the trim of the spinnaker, the shape of the sail and the amount of wind. The tack, attached to the pole, should be kept at the same height,and to do this the outboard end of the pole must be moved up or down as appropriate. With a good breeze, the wind in the sail will tend to lift the pole, so to raise the pole it is necessary only to ease the foreguy and the outboard end will rise.

If there is little wind, the pole's own weight will be pulling it and the spinnaker downwards, and the pole end must then be adjusted on the topping lift, remembering first to slacken the foreguy to allow the pole end to lift. To lower the tack, first ease the topping lift. If the pole does not drop by its own weight, it will have to be winched down with the downhaul or foreguy.

Pole height - inboard end

With the outboard end set, the inboard end must be moved to keep the pole horizontal: this keeps the outboard end of the spinnaker as far away from the mast as possible, thus giving the maximum projected area of sail. Ideally the pole should be horizontal or slightly cocked upwards. If the pole is allowed to get too far out of horizontal, especially if the outboard end is below the level of the inboard end, there is a danger of the inward thrusting forces on the end of the pole causing it to capsize, the inboard end scooting up to the stopper on the top end of the mast track, and the outer end slamming down onto the deck. Naturally, this does not apply to small yachts with only a fixed ring attachment at the mast for the pole.

Pole height - keep it rigid

Every time the pole height is adjusted the foreguy and the topping lift must be tightened up to keep the pole end rigid under the tack of the spinnaker. If the pole end is allowed to slop about, all it does is

Sunsail Sun Fast 36

shake the air out of the spinnaker.
Conversely, remember always to ease the
foreguy before trying to move the inboard
end of the pole. This will reduce the
inward-thrusting forces and take the weight
off the pole and the slider on the mast track.

RULES FOR RUNNING

Straight downwind, or very broad
reaching, the yacht stays more or less
upright and the spinnaker is at its best,
virtually all its power being used to pull the
yacht along, little being used in heeling her
over or dragging her sideways.

Weight aft

Because it is attached near the top of the
mast, the spinnaker pulling forward on the
yacht well above the waterline exerts a
turning force which acts to push the bows
down into the water. For this reason, the
harder it blows the more weight there has
to be aft to help lift the bows; running fast
downwind in a blow, virtually all the crew

*Weight should be moved aft as the wind gets
stronger. You don't want anyone up on the
bows if you can help it.*

move aft, sometimes aft of the helmsman.

Preventing rolling

Rolling is the biggest problem when sailing
straight downwind under spinnaker,
particularly in heavy airs and big seas
when things can become so bad that the
boat becomes unmanageable. As well as
the obvious effects of hurling everyone off
their feet and smashing the crockery down
below, heavy rolling makes the boat very
difficult to steer because of the rapid and
dramatic changes to the immersed shape.

   The rolling is caused largely by the
spinnaker being badly trimmed, and in
particular by the sail being too full aloft.
When this happens the top of the spinnaker
starts to sway from side to side, pulling on
first one side of the mast, then the other and
acting like a giant pendulum. As the wind
strengthens the spinnaker has to be

flattened to take some of the power out of its shoulders. This is done by leading the sheet and guy from progressively further forward, until they are both led through blocks almost up at the shrouds. In this way, the two corners of the sail are pulled down, narrowing and flattening the head of the sail.

Trimming out of a roll

You can damp and even stop the roll simply by trimming. As the boat rolls to windward, trim on both the spinnaker and the mainsail. As she starts the other way, ease both sheets. With good co-ordinated trimming you can stop a roll almost before it starts - and on some boats this spells the difference between staying upright and wiping-out spectacularly. On a twitchy grand prix racer like the Mumm 36, for instance, you get one, maybe two rolls before the pole end goes in the water, and

then the boat trips round the end of the pole and gybe-broaches in a quite spectacular manner.

Moving the leads

On many big boats now, dinghy practice has been adopted with a permanently rigged trimming line fitted about midships, with the tail led to a purchase or winch and the spinnaker sheet rove permanently through the block at the outboard end. This is used to adjust the angle of the spinnaker sheet to the sail. Pulling the trim-line on has the effect of moving the sheet lead block forward, making the angle between sheet and sail more vertical and thus pulling the spinnaker clew more down than aft. Letting the trim-line off effectively moves the sheet lead aft, rendering the pull of the sheet on the sail more horizontal (aft) than downwards. In boats without trim lines, we lead the sheet from its turning block by the

Trimming the spinnaker and mainsail is the way to stop a downwind roll. If you let the boat roll too far, it loses speed, stresses the crew, and frequently ends in a wipe-out. A good crew prevents it before it starts.

winch to the sail through a movable lead-block (usually a snatch block, in case at some stage we want to take the sheet right out of the block without unreaving the whole thing). We use this to alter the sheet lead angle.

In lighter winds the leads are moved by clipping a block to the toerail forward of the spinnaker turning block or permanent sheet lead, and pulling the sheet down and into the snatch block by brute force. In stronger winds, brute force will not be enough and cunning must be used. The lazy guy and the lazy sheet are simple and ideal tools to use when moving spinnaker leads. Rig the new lead block for the spinnaker sheet in the desired position - using a snatch block - with another just ahead of it. Rig the lazy guy, which of course has no weight on it, through the forward block and take the weight of the sail on it, either on a free winch or direct to a cleat. Now let the weight right off the sheet, rig it through the new block, take the turns on the winch again, and take the weight of the sail back onto the sheet. Finally take the lazy guy out of the move block. The same technique can be used with the lazy sheet to move the lead of the guy.

Re-trimming the flatter sail

As the leads are moved forward, so the corners of the sail move downwards, requiring the pole to be lowered to keep the tack and clew at the same height. It can pay now to have the pole slightly forward of its normal setting, and to de-power the spinnaker by oversheeting. Too much power and the energy is used up in making the yacht roll.

RULES FOR REACHING

The reaching spinnaker is flatter than the running spinnaker, either by virtue of different trimming technique and leads, or by being a different sail. For reaching the guy will normally be led forward, usually at the point of maximum beam of the yacht, while the sheet will lead from further aft. It is illegal under the racing rules to lead the sheet through the end of the main boom or through an out-rigger. Both the foot and head of the sail must be flatter than for running to reduce the heeling moment; when shy reaching – that is with the apparent wind forward of the beam - the sail is acting more like a genoa than a running spinnaker.

Pole and tack height

When broad or beam reaching, tack and clew should be the same height (as for running), and this height will be dictated by the free-flying clew. As the apparent wind moves forward, the pole can be used to set the height of the corners of the sail and the clew made to follow. Shy reaching, we want the tack of the sail low, to lengthen the apparent length of the luff – the projected length – and to straighten the luff and flatten the sail, again to lessen the heeling moment. The pole can be bowsed down on the foreguy (lowering the mast end to match), and the clew barber-hauled down to the required height.

9 Gybing the Spinnaker

Gybing the spinnaker should be a manoeuvre which holds no greater terror for the good crew than does tacking. The type of gear with which the yacht is fitted will to a great extent dictate the method by which the spinnaker is handled. With the double-ended pole both end-for-end gybes and dip-pole gybes are possible.

The usual errors

Although it is inevitably the poor foredeck hand who gets the blame when a gybe goes badly, many of the errors in gybing actually occur in trimming or in calling the gybe. If the pole is tripped a fraction too early, the spinnaker will lift and roll and probably collapse - or cause exciting control problems on the helm. Call the trip too late, and the spinnaker is drawing too far over what was the windward side, trying to pull the guy sideways and the pole-end will not drop free.   If the guy is pulled on too quickly, you pull the foredeck hand aft with it; too late and it either wraps around the pole, or the pole crashes into the headfoil, or both. Top the pole too early and it goes out through the front of the spinnaker, too late and it catches under the guardrails. Clear calls of "Trip!" to start the gybe sequence and, from the foredeck, "Made!" when the guy is in and you are out of the way, are also important.

DOUBLE ENDED POLE: END-FOR-END GYBE ON THE RUN

This is the method used with smaller spinnakers. The pole fittings at each end are identical; the pole is supported by a topping lift led to a wire span or bridle, so that held only by the topping lift the pole would appear to hang on a sling. Single lines to the spinnaker are used, each line acting as both the sheet and the guy, depending on where the pole is. In the end-for-end gybe, the pole in effect moves horizontally across the boat, the inboard end becoming the outboard end and vice versa.

Personnel

Two people are needed to look after the spinnaker, one on the foredeck and one in the cockpit who looks after both sheet and guy. In addition, there must be someone to gybe the mainsail and someone to look after the runners. There should be someone steering the yacht – no kidding, the helmsman is a important member of the gybing team. The boat should be steered as straight downwind as possible; it is particularly important not to luff up on the new gybe while the spinnaker is still being handled. *The Golden Rule is Keep her under the Chute.*

The gybe least likely to go wrong is the gybe from one side to the other while

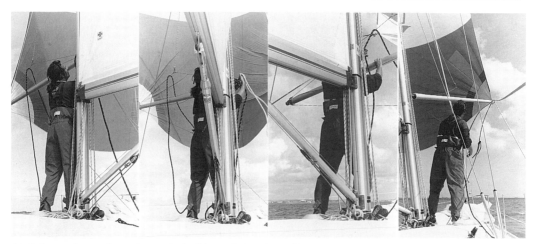

End-for-end seen from the cockpit: The pole is taken off the mast and taken across the boat, clipped to the new guy, and clipped back onto the mast as the old guy drops off. Remember to pass the 'new' (starboard side) genoa sheet over the pole as you're doing this.

square running or very broad reaching. Here is how it goes.

Foredeck

Before even going onto the foredeck, ensure that the pole is set at a height where it can be reached without climbing: ideally it should be at shoulder height. Then ease the foreguy slightly: not enough to allow the pole to go out of control, but enough to take the tension off it and the pole. The foreguy, when hard on, forces the pole end against the mast and if not eased before the gybe, the pole, mast, foreguy and topping lift act like a giant bow and arrow so that the pole flies off the mast as soon as the catch is released. Even if this does not happen, the foredeck hand will have a very hard task pushing out against the foreguy to set the pole on the other gybe. So ease the foreguy before you start.

Once on the foredeck make sure the leeward genoa sheet is within easy reach, if necessary by holding it in the crook of your elbow. Stand at the mast, on the weather side, facing forwards. Many crews start to handle the pole standing in front of the mast facing aft: but they find halfway through the gybe they have to change position to complete the operation. If you work facing forwards, you are watching the spinnaker the whole time, are in greater control of what is happening, and can exert more of whatever strength you have.

Once the word "Go!" is given, unclip the pole, move with it round the front of the mast, and at the same time slip the slack (new) windward genoa sheet over the end. Pull the pole (hanging on the topping-lift bridle, so there is no weight on it) across and grab the spinnaker sheet just forward of the shroud. Clip the pole upwards onto the spinnaker sheet (on all yacht spinnaker systems, the pole is used with the open jaw of the end fitting facing upwards) and continue pushing the pole out, at the same time sliding it forwards along what has now become the guy towards the corner of the spinnaker.

While doing this, pull the release line to

the other end of the pole and flick that end downwards, allowing what was the guy and is now the sheet to ride up clear of the pole. Make sure the old genoa sheet has dropped off this end of the pole. Continue to push the pole across and clip it up into the ring on the mast. The spinnaker has been gybed.

In light weather

A smoother gybe results if, once the pole is unclipped from the mast, it is unclipped from the old guy before being clipped to the new guy. The spinnaker floats wide and clear, without the danger of a collapse being brought on by the two corners being pulled together by the relatively short spinnaker pole. However, there comes a point as the wind increases where to do this is unsafe, as the spinnaker can take charge.

Meanwhile, back aft

The sheet and guy are used to fly the spinnaker like a giant kite, gently bringing it round the forestay as the yacht turns beneath it. If the run was square, what was the guy and is now to be the sheet will be too far aft, while what is becoming the guy will be too far forward - too much eased. On a small yacht sheet and guy are held by one person. The most usual cause of collapse is failing to ease the new sheet enough, so the sail stays to leeward where it soon starves of air. Easing the sheet will let the spinnaker float high and free; bring the guy back only after the inboard end has been made, otherwise all you are doing is turning the foredeck hand into an archer, trying to push a giant arrow back against the taut bowstring of the guy.

The main should be gybed at the moment the inboard end of the pole is

clipped onto the new guy, thus keeping the flow of air to the spinnaker as unimpeded as possible. It can help to hold the main on the centreline for a moment, thus giving the spinnaker maximum air. The yacht should be steered to stay at all times underneath the spinnaker.

Runners

In light and medium winds release the old runner, and bring on the new runner just as the main comes across.In heavy weather, pull the main in to the centreline, bring on the new runner, let off the old runner, gybe and then let the main out on the new side. Note that it is always more important to let the old runner off than to pull the new one on: the boom must not hit the old runner as it swings across as this could carry away the entire rig.

On a yacht where the runners are led right aft the length of the boom determines whether the runners go under the boom or stay over the top, around the back of the mainsail leech. With a long boom (i.e. the boom end would hit the runner when fully made up) they stay under. Shockcord should have been rigged from the spreader root to the runner at about half-height to pull the runner forward as soon as it is slackened. With a short boom, shockcords are often rigged from about one-third of the way up the backstay to near the runner end or checkstay block, to pull the runner up and out of the way as soon as it is slackened, with the slackened runner lying over the boom and pulling round the back of the mainsail. Joining a new boat, the way in which the shockcord is rigged will tell you which way the runners should go when you gybe.

End for end seen from off the boat. The spinnaker should be controlled from the two sheets throughout, flown high and clear of the mainsail by easing both sheets a little. Keeping the sheets over-trimmed usually collapses the spinnaker in the lee of the mainsail. The main is centred and then flipped across and the helmsman steers to keep the yacht under her spinnaker.

Mainsail

The main can be pulled across by hand in light weather, but as the breeze increases it must be trimmed in on the sheet to close-hauled, gybed, and then eased out on the sheet. Just when the change is made depends on the size of mainsail: on big mainsails, the sheet should always be used. On a fractional boat the main plays a vital role at a crucial moment in the gybe: it holds the mast up. The main traveller should be centred for the gybe; as the boat turns the new runner cannot be made until the boom is out of the way, so hold the mainsheet hard with the boom on the centreline until you are sure the new runner has the weight, then let it run.

The helmsman must stop the turn as soon as the mainsail flicks into its new shape, but before the sail is truly full. If the turn is continued too quickly with the main held amidships, the main fills, heels the boat, and within a twinkling she has wiped-out to weather. Happily this stricture coincides directly with the rule of steering the boat so as to keep her under the spinnaker.

DOUBLE-ENDED POLE - DIP-POLE GYBE REACH TO REACH

Gybing from a shy reach to a shy reach the end-for-end method can be used, but as the reaches become shyer, greater difficulty is experienced in keeping everything under control and, in particular, in clipping the pole back onto the mast. The normal way of coping is simply to run square for a bit, do a normal gybe, and then sharpen up.   The old-style Olympic course had a shy reach-to-reach gybe at the apex of the triangle leg, and here you would lose much time and space and many places as you ran off. Occasionally you may find yourself still sailing that old-style course - so here is how to do the dip-pole gybe without having to rig lazy sheets and guys.

For this the mast end of the pole has to be on a track which allows it to ride up the front of the mast. It must go high enough to allow the outer end of the pole to swing down on the topping-lift bridle and come in under the forestay. The pole is then raised to horizontal by dropping the mast end to

its former position.

Foredeck

Ease the foreguy, go forward. As the yacht bears away into the gybe, trip the guy out of the pole end by pulling the string, and at the same time hit the underside of the pole at the mast end hard with the heel of your hand. This will send the inboard end up the mast and capsize the pole, leaving it hanging in the topping-lift bridle so that the outboard end points down at the foredeck. Swing the end round behind the forestay (and in between the genoa sheets, to put the other one over the pole end), then pull down on the mast end to tip the pole back to horizontal. As the yacht gybes, the spinnaker is trimmed to swing across the front of the forestay, bringing what will now be the guy to the pole end. Clip on. Move back aft and re-set the foreguy.

Meanwhile, back aft

The spinnaker trimmer is very important in this gybe. As the yacht gybes the spinnaker must be trimmed (hauling in the new sheet, easing away the new guy) to move the sail round to meet the pole end. In particular the new guy has to be over-eased past its proper setting, to allow it to be clipped to the pole. Then it must be trimmed back to the correct setting. Make sure the foredeck hand has all the guy required. Although not used so much on offshore boats now, this technique still works well in deliciously old-fashioned boats like the Dragon and the Etchells 22.

SINGLE-ENDED POLE - DIP-POLE TECHNIQUE

By definition, a single-ended pole can only be gybed by the dip-pole technique, since the mast end always stays on the mast. Lazy sheets and guys are also always used. More elaborate preparation is required than for the simpler double-ended pole end-for-end gybe, and a bigger team is needed, since there are more jobs to be done and the gear is that much heavier.

Personnel

- A foredeck hand, who works mainly in the pulpit.
- A mast hand, working at the mast.
- Someone on the topping lift and foreguy.
- Someone on the sheet and guy, each side (in light weather or smaller yachts, this can be one person doing both sides).
- Someone on the runners, if fitted.
- Someone on the mainsheet.
- And, of course, the helmsman.

Making ready

Let us not forget the `five peas': Proper Preparation Prevents Poor Performance.

The staysail, if set, must first be handed and out of the way. The headsail, which will usually be already down and on the deck, should be bagged and taken off, or tied down low to permit the pole end to swing down behind the forestay and through the foretriangle. This may mean you have to take the headsail out of the pre-feeder and even the luff groove altogether. It is a wise precaution to take one of the spare halyards, stowed on the mast, and clip it on the pulpit: this ensures that when the gybe is over, we do not end up with all the spare halyards on the wrong side of the spinnaker pole.

Take the genoa sheets off the genoa and tie them together. This keeps them led correctly over the pole, and they can be untied and reattached to the genoa when needed. The babystay, if there is one, must be unshipped and taken back to the mast, otherwise the spinnaker pole cannot swing across the foredeck. The lazy guy (which is about to become the working guy) should be pulled well forward into the pulpit, but led the way it will lead when working - there should not be any loops in it, to keep life simple in the hurried moments of the actual gybe.

Make sure that the lazy sheet is over the top of the pole end, so that the pole, when tripped, can swing freely downwards, away from the old guy. Also check that a strop (usually a sail tie) has been rigged to the toggle on the tripping line of the pole, to enable it to be reached with the pole raised up the mast. Finally, make sure everyone knows what they have to do: if necessary the crew boss should talk the whole operation through.

Foredeck

The foredeck hand should be positioned in the pulpit, ahead of the forestay, facing aft. The mast hand raises the inboard end of the pole on its track to the mark that indicates the pole end is high enough to allow the outboard end to drop down and under the forestay, then trips the pole by pulling on the tripping line to open the jaw at the outboard end, releasing the guy. The spinnaker will lift the guy out and clear of the pole end. If the sail is reluctant, drawing in the new sheet while easing the old guy will usually cure the problem.

The pulpit hand hauls in on the foreguy as the pole end is lowered on the topping lift. Guide the pole end down and under the forestay, either dropping the unwanted genoa sheet off the end and slipping the new genoa sheet over the end as the pole comes through or, if the advice about unbuttoning the sheets and tying them together has been followed, making sure the joined-together sheets do not drop off the end of the pole. As the pole swings under the forestay, call for the topping lift to raise the pole again, at the same time leading the new guy correctly through the jaw at the pole end and snapping the plunger closed - keeping your finger out of the way. Check to see there are no snags with the genoa sheet or the foreguy as the pole is topped up and the sail retrimmed.

The mast hand lowers the inboard end of the pole to the correct height for proper spinnaker trim. This done, the two on the foredeck should gybe the genoa which is lying on deck by pulling it round the foreguy and leading it down the new leeward side, so that it is ready for hoisting if needed. If the yacht is close reaching, the babystay must be set up again. It will now be on the wrong side of the pole, and have to be led over the topping lift. With a really good crew, all this mast and foredeck work can be done by one man, even on a 45-footer (13.5m).

Mainsail and runners

Treat exactly as dealt with earlier in this chapter, bearing in mind that the mainsail on this size of yacht will be too big to be handled casually: it must always be handled on the sheet. The main traveller should always be centred and cleated off - it should not be allowed to fly across the track unchecked. Sooner or later it just hits the end-stop and keeps going. Slick runner work is vital, since on a reach-to-reach

gybe the mainsail cannot be used to support the mast: as the boat turns on to her new course, the mainsail must be eased, or a broach will result.

Golden Rule: Keep air in the spinnaker. Trim the main amidships quickly at the start of the gybe (this helps the runner-man get the new runner on in good time), then gybe the main boom as the pole comes across. This keeps most of the spinnaker working in clear air and helps keep it full and flying. If the main is gybed late, it blankets the spinnaker which then collapses, causing all sorts of problems as it wraps itself round the head of the person in the pulpit and over the end of the pole.

Dip-pole gybe, run to run. Trip the sail (1), dip the pole and clip on the new guy (2). Raise the pole and gybe the main (3); winch the pole aft (4) and trim the sail(5).

10 Changing the Spinnaker

We now learn why the yacht is blessed with more than one spinnaker halyard: she carries anything up to five different spinnakers, each designed with a different task in mind, made from different weights of cloth and constructed in different ways.

PEELING
Inside/outside

The usual method of changing spinnakers on a racing yacht is the peel, developed, like most racing crewing techniques, to lose as little speed as possible during the work. Done perfectly, the peel will lose no speed at all, since in essence it involves setting the new spinnaker inside the existing spinnaker, getting the new sail drawing, and then releasing the tack of the old sail so that it peels away from the

swelling face of the new sail like a layer of onion skin to flutter briefly, flag-like, before being spirited away. This is the simple inside hoist/outside drop, the classic peel - and sometimes it actually works like that, too.

Outside/inside

Less neat is the opposite version, the outside hoist/inside drop, where the new sail goes up outside the old sail, is filled and got drawing, and the old taken down inside the curve of the new sail. It seldom works like that, because as the new spinnaker goes up it tends to upset and collapse the old spinnaker, and it cannot really find the air to fill until the old sail is down and out of the way.

Why then ever do an outside hoist? The

The new spinnaker is hoisted quickly on the inside, and then set with the sheet while being held at the tack by the peeling strop. The clip on the end of the guy is then transferred from old tack to new tack, the peeling strop unclipped, and the old sail dropped onto the deck under the foot of the new spinnaker. Semi-collapse by both sails during the manoeuvre (as shown here) should ideally be avoided.

position of the halyards dictates which technique is employed, for the halyards must not be crossed at any stage during the change. So if the existing spinnaker is up on the windward halyard (spinnaker on starboard halyard with the boat on starboard gybe, or port halyard with the boat on port gybe), an outside leeward hoist has to be used. This, however, is a case of one rule for the good and another rule for the even better. To overcome the problems of the outside hoist the slickest crews do cross the halyards and use an inside hoist; then immediately send a man aloft to change the halyards over and undo the cross. We shall come to that later.

Peeling equipment

Only one pole is used throughout a peel, but we need a sheet and guy for the new spinnaker in addition to the sheet and guy on the spinnaker already flying. As sheet, we normally will use the lazy guy off the sail already set as a changing sheet, and to act as a temporary guy a short length of line with a spinnaker clip on the end is used. This is called a peeling strop which should be tied in the pulpit, usually to the stem-head fitting or to the forestay or headfoil itself. For this, use a rolling hitch so that the strop does not slide up the forestay. Hitch the strop to the forestay itself under the

Rigging a peeling strop. The clip will go into the spinnaker tack, led to weather of the forestay.

bottom piece of the headfoil, rather than round the headfoil if possible, to avoid the risk of crushing the headfoil. The clip goes straight onto the spinnaker tack, led to weather of the forestay.

The length of the strop should be such as to allow the new spinnaker to set with the tack just above the height of the pulpit, but near the forestay. Once set, and with the old sail released, the guy will be pulled through the pole end to be clipped to the tack of the new sail, so this must be in easy reach of the crew member working in the pulpit.

Peeling without a strop

With a nimble bowman (and a pole end that will take two guys) we can do without the peeling strop. We use the new guy rigged through the pole end, put there by the bowman and brought back on deck to be buttoned on to the new spinnaker. The tack is then hauled out to the pole end before we hoist, just in the way in which we cheat the guy when doing an ordinary hoist.

Daredevil bowmen will take the new tack out to the pole end, swinging out on a halyard or climbing up the foreguy to clip themselves to the pole. The new tack is clipped direct to the pole or to a very short strop at the pole-end before the hoist, then the bowman remains at the pole end during the hoist, trips the old sail and transfers the guy to the new sail at the pole end, then comes down and in to a well-earned round of applause.

PEELING TECHNIQUE

Let's take a simple situation as an example. The yacht is broad reaching under the half-ounce spinnaker on starboard gybe. The wind is showing signs of increasing in strength, and drawing ahead; already there

has been one near broach as a stronger than usual gust came through. We decide to change to the slightly smaller and flatter cut 30/20, which will be a better sail for these conditions. The half-ounce is set on the port halyard, so it will be an inside hoist/outside drop. We have the sheet and lazy guy rigged on the existing sail, with the guy and lazy sheet on the other (starboard) side.

Making ready

The new sail is brought on deck still packed in its turtle, the three corners ready for clipping on. Unclip the lazy guy from the clew of the existing spinnaker (help may be needed here to pull the sheet downwards and inboard, to allow the clips to be reached). Clip on the lazy guy as sheet to the new sail.

Take the tack of the new sail forward to the peeling strop already hitched to the forestay and clip on. Alternatively, the bowman goes out to the pole end, drops the sheet into the beak, and the weight of the existing spinnaker having been transferred to the sheet he unclips the unloaded guy and brings its end back down, leaving it rove through the beak.

Unclip the starboard spinnaker halyard from its stowed position (probably on the mast) and check its lead, visualising how the head of the sail will travel aloft when the time comes to hoist. If the halyard has been stowed normally, it will have to be taken forward and round the forestay, so that it leads over the top of the forestay, before being brought aft and clipped to the new spinnaker.

We are ready to go

To peel the spinnaker we will need:

• Someone on the halyards, to pull the

new sail up and secure the halyard, then let the old halyard go to lower the old sail.

- Someone on the sheets (port side) to set the new sail and to throw the sheet of the old sail off the winch.
- People to gather in the old sail.
- Someone on the guy (starboard side) to ease the pole forward to where the foredeck hand can release the guy, and to let the guy on forward to collect the new sail.
- Possibly someone on the topping lift to ensure that the pole is low enough for the foredeck hand to reach everthing.

Foredeck

The foredeck hand has a busy time during a peel. You must:

- Make the new spinnaker ready and clip it on.
- Move back to the mast to hand-haul the spinnaker halyard to hoist the new sail, while the tailer takes the halyard up on the winch.
- Move forward and possibly climb up in the pulpit to release the tack of the old sail, then pull the guy through the pole end to the new sail.
- Then move aft again to help gather in the old sail as it comes down.

The hoist

When all is ready the new spinnaker is hoisted smartly, the foredeck hand hauling on the halyard at the mast, the tailer taking the halyard onto the winch. Once the sail is up, the sheet is taken in until the sail fills and begins to set. With the tack of the sail on the peeling strop, there is nothing for the guy hand to do, until...

The changeover

With the new sail up, let the pole go forward until the foredeck hand can release the tack of the old sail. He should keep his head out of the way, lest the pole springs back as the load comes off. The guy must now be eased further, so that the foredeck hand can take it down and clip it to the tack of the new sail. When the guy is clipped on, the foredeck hand calls aft and unclips the peeling strop, and the guy hand hauls in the guy to bring the tack to the pole, then trims the pole to where it should be.

The drop

As the old sail flags out, the old sheet must be hauled in from as far forward as possible, the foot of the sail gathered, and the halyard let go for the old sail to be gathered. Handing the spinnaker is dealt with fully in the next chapter, which if nothing else demonstrates the wisdom of reading the whole book before trying any of the individual moves described.

Meanwhile, back aft

Yet again, it is teamwork which counts and we have already seen how the action shifts quickly from the foredeck to the cockpit and back again. Everyone must watch everyone else and stay with what is going on. Of those back aft, the guy hand in particular is crucial to the slickness of the operation, having to let the pole forward by the right amount at the right moment, pause while the foredeck hand releases the old sail, then let the guy on forward so that the foredeck hand can attach it to the tack of the new sail.

Variations - outside hoist

Had the half-ounce in our example been up on the starboard halyard, the 30/20 would have had to go up on the port halyard. In this case the port halyard would be taken from its stowage on the mast, the lead checked aloft, and the halyard led outside the sheet of the half-ounce and back over the top of the guardrail to the head of the 30/20.

With an outside hoist, the pole should be let forward right to the forestay before the old sail is released; this will prevent it blowing out round the luff of the new sail before it can be lowered. The outside hoist goes much better if the strop is dispensed with, and the guy unloaded and used as described earlier.

UNCROSSING HALYARDS

In the course of a long, dark and fickle night, with two or three watch changes, there might routinely be two or three spinnaker peels; on one of those sloppy, frustrating nights that make you wonder what's so very wrong with spending the night in bed there might be many more. Sooner or later it is realised that the halyards have become crossed, usually by using the wrong ploy.

The halyard is uncrossed by leading it outside the spinnaker which is up. Because of the shape of the sail at the top (where it will be almost horizontal), and because of the great belly of cloth beneath this horizontal top, this is a tricky business. The first question to ask is "Can we safely leave it?". If the next mark is close ahead, with a beat to follow, and the spinnaker that`s up can be got down (possibly having to let both halyards go), the answer is "Yes"; and the mess can be sorted out much more easily without a sail in the way. If the answer is "No", the halyard has to be retrieved.

Uncrossing technique

A light line is attached to the working end of the halyard, and the halyard led forward to go round outside the sail. Take the line aft along the bottom of the sail and try pulling the halyard round. On no account force it, for the risk of snagging and tearing the spinnaker is great. If it won't come with the sail full, try collapsing the sail briefly by letting out the sheet very quickly, pulling the line as the sail flaps. This might sound drastic, but the sail need be collapsed only momentarily, and eight times out of ten the halyard will fall freely past the sail.

The other two times are when there is more than one cross in the halyards. Here, the simplest solution might be to go up and get the halyard. Rig the bosun's chair and send the lightest crew member aloft. Up there, apart from having a fabulous view, the halyard can be pulled up and through the cross and the end dropped back down again with a clear lead. This might sound drastic - but in the end it can prove the quickest method and less detrimental to speed than the on-going distraction of a full-fledged committee meeting on the foredeck while assorted pet theories are tried and discarded.

Going aloft

Increasingly, the better crews have bowmen who do not flinch at the thought of going aloft: indeed, no serious grand-prix level racer fiddles about with trying to uncross halyards from the deck, and the bowman dons his climbing harness at the start of the race the way the dinghy crew dons his trapeze harness.

Safety is paramount. Always have two

Top boats are well used to sending a 'monkey' aloft to deal with problems such as crossed halyards. The ideal is to avoid them in the first place

people on the halyard which takes the man aloft. The man climbing can speed the uplift by pulling himself up the rigging - but the halyard tailers must keep up with the climb, lest the winch become over-rode or, with slack in the climbing halyard, the man aloft slips and starts to drop.

Going aloft, never rely on a halyard clip to take your weight. Have a shackle on the front eye of the climbing harness, and shackle the harness through the hard eye of the halyard. In rough weather, a retrieving line from the harness clip to a trusted friend on deck is a good idea, both to steady you up aloft and bring you safely the last and most difficult few feet from boom and guardrail height back on to the deck.

Going out to the pole-end, really good bowmen hand-over-hand up the foreguy, then clip themselves on briefly when they get there to leave both hands free to work. But this is a book primarily for those just taking to big boat crewing - by the time

you have served your apprenticeship you will have seen for yourself the way the top crews work.

BARE-HEADED CHANGING

Not every spinnaker change has to be done by peeling. It is sometimes better to take one spinnaker off before putting the next one up: the only criterion being which method will lose the yacht the least speed. In heavy weather something going wrong can lose a great deal of time, even if it does not become actually dangerous; with the boat going at near her maximum speed under mainsail alone, it might be both safer and ultimately quicker to hand one spinnaker before replacing it with another. In very light weather, the inevitable disturbance of peeling, even with everyone creeping about on tiptoe and conversing in whispers, might slow the boat more than the brief loss of speed from a bare-headed change.

11 Handing the Spinnaker

Before the spinnaker is taken off it is necessary to decide what is going to happen next (yacht races are won by thinking ahead) - so the correct headsail must be set before the spinnaker is handed. There is another, more prosaic, reason for setting the headsail: it is a great deal easier to get the spinnaker down behind the shelter of the headsail, than to get it down while it is still full of wind. The required headsail may be anything from the high-clewed reacher to the number three genoa: it should be brought on deck, and any other headsail (left over from the previous leg) cleared away.

'HANDING' THE SPINNAKER

There are several methods of 'handing' the spinnaker, but all have a common aim: to transform that mighty, controlled giant,

which is harmless enough when under control and pulling like a steam loco, into an equally harmless pile of empty, and preferably dry, nylon, safely below deck; and to do it with the minimum of fuss and in the shortest possible time. The longer the time taken over this transformation, the greater the chance of something going wrong.

The first Golden Rule of spinnaker handing is *Get the wind out of it*; the second Golden Rule is *Don't drop it, bring it down*.

The halyard, the sheet, the guy and the spinnaker

Handing the spinnaker, all three lines to the sail play vital roles. Bringing the sail down is, quite literally, the reverse of putting it up. In the basic racing technique, used in winds of more than 10mph, the trick is to ease the pole forward to the forestay but

Once the genoa is up and driving the spinnaker halyard is let go. The sail is smartly hauled in under the boom as the guy is eased off, and taken down through the companionway. The quicker this is all done the less speed will be lost by the spinnaker flapping, and the less chance there is of dropping it over the side.

keep tension on both sheet and guy - the guy particularly - and dump the halyard. Contrary to the laws of physics the sail will not fall in the water. Instead, the head of the sail blows away to leeward, instantly de-powering the straining giant, and the sail wafts gently o'er the waves like a huge horizontal pennon.

The sail can now be grabbed in the middle of the taut foot, and the floating nylon swiftly gathered. The quicker the main body of the sail is gathered, the less likely any of it is to go in the water. With the first armfuls of the sail in hand the sheet can be released, making the gathering easier and quicker. With half the sail inboard, the guy can be slackened and the whole sail bundled down inside the guardrails onto the foredeck, into the cockpit or down the forehatch, depending on the size and configuration of the yacht. Curiously, the harder it is blowing the easier it is to use this technique.

Personnel

- Someone on the guy, to let the pole forward.
- Someone on the foredeck, to gather the sail.
- Someone on the sheet, to ease when ready then help gather the sail.
- Someone on the halyard, to lower the sail.

Organisation

On a big boat, there will usually be at least one person for each job, plus a couple of spare hands to gather in the sail. On a small boat (say with only four in the crew counting the helmsman), some people will have to do more than one job.

- The hand on the guy eases the pole forward, then if there is no separate pit man moves to the halyard.
- The foredeck hand gathers the spinnaker.
- The sheet hand starts hauling sheet as soon as the sail is eased to bring the foot taut along the back of the headsail and so the foredeck hand can grab it, then eases sheet as the sail is gathered.
- The guy hand or pit man dumps the halyard once the foot of the sail is pulled taut.
- The foredeck hand bundles the sail down and away. The pit man helps get it down the main hatch.

As the yacht hardens round the mark, mainsheet, traveller and genoa sheet must be tended. On a big boat there will be the luxury of separate people for each job; on a small boat, whoever does the mainsheet can do the guy for the drop, then get back on the mainsheet for the rounding, while the spinnaker sheet trimmer moves to the genoa.

The foredeck hand ties on the genoa sheets ensuring they are over the top of the pole and its bridle. The genoa goes up as the yacht bears away, with the foredeck hand helping on the halyard.

Golden Rule: The Foot of the sail must be Pulled Taut Before the Halyard is Dumped. This is how the horizontal flag effect is achieved. Dumping the halyard with the sheet and guy still in their sailing positions simply lets the whole sail go slack and it falls in the water. At best this looks very ordinary, at worst the yacht runs over the spinnaker which then snags around the keel and possibly the rudder too.

VARIATIONS ON A THEME

Mostly for bigger boats - 33ft (10m) and above - with bigger spinnakers.

FOREDECK DROP FROM REACH

The sail is brought down behind and under the genoa, to be gathered on the foredeck and (usually but not necessarily) bundled straight down the forehatch.
Simultaneously with the halyard being dumped, the tack of the sail is pulled in and down behind the genoa using the lazy sheet or a line rigged specially for the

purpose. The sheet is held until the bulk of the sail is gathered.

Personnel

Much as for the standard drop. On a boat with a big spinnaker an extra person will be needed on the foredeck to gather the sail, and on yachts over 36ft (11m) someone usually goes below the open forehatch, to act as long stop on the lazy sheet or recovery line and to gather the sail as it is bundled through the hatch.

Method

On a yacht with single guy and sheet fasten a spare length of line, heavy enough to be handled under load without cutting hands, to the tack of the sail. Lead this forward and round the forestay to leeward of the genoa, over the top of and inside the pulpit and guardrails and under the foot of the genoa. Secure the end to something substantial, like the mast. Alternatively you can use the lazy sheet (if there is one), either by unreeving it from the lead blocks aft or by taking a bight forward, if there is enough line: make sure there is plenty of slack in the lazy sheet to bring it well back on the foredeck.

On the word to hand the sail, ease the guy forward until the pole is on the forestay, the foredeck hand taking in the slack on the lazy sheet or retrieval line. When the pole is on the forestay, keep the guy going out, fast but sensibly, until all the weight is transferred to the foredeck hand or team hauling on the retrieval line. (This is to stop the pole crashing against and wrecking the headfoil, which is what happens if you simply dump the guy.) Once they have the weight, the guy hand throws the guy right off the winch and makes sure it is clear to be pulled through. This should all happen a good deal faster than the time it takes to read about it.

As the tack comes in behind and under the genoa, the luff of the spinnaker pulls taut, backfills and the sail collapses at which point the halyard can be dumped. The sheet can finally be let go once the spinnaker is coming in under the genoa, so that foot and the upper part of the luff are handed together, while the sheet hand trims the genoa sheet.

Advantages

This is a very fast method when done correctly, and by bringing the sail down behind the genoa the drop can be left much later. Indeed it is almost an advantage to leave everything late, for the spinnaker falls behind both genoa and main and is virtually blown inboard by the flow of air building up across the back of the genoa as the yacht comes on the wind. The pole can stay up, safe against the forestay, as the yacht rounds up round the mark, to be taken down later (thus saving precious seconds).

This method can only be used when leaving the mark to the windward side; leaving the mark to leeward - and thus having to gybe round it - an early drop or a full float drop has to be used.

FORDECK DROP FROM RUN

Use the same method of bringing the spinnaker down, but instead of bringing it in to leeward under the genoa, bring the retrieval line or bight of the lazy sheet straight down onto the deck from the end of the squared-off pole, and thus bring the sail in to weather of the forestay and genoa.

Method

Ease the guy to transfer the weight to the retrieval line, and at the same time dump the sheet completely to empty the sail - which would otherwise remain full. The halyard can be let go allowing the sail to fall onto the foredeck - the boat virtually sails underneath the falling spinnaker - but take care that the sail does not fall over the bow and into the water, to be run down by the boat. That really slows things up.

FLOAT DROP

A float drop is simply taking the pole off and putting it away before taking the spinnaker down, leaving the spinnaker to float free and continue drawing while this is done. It can thus only be done square or very broad to the wind. It is quite legal - contrary to folklore you do not have to carry a pole with the spinnaker (the rule was changed 'way back in 1992, but rule changes sometimes take awhile to filter this far forward). A float drop is often used in light weather when no gybe is involved. But in any wind strength it is very useful if a gybe drop is needed, in other words if the

Float drop: On the run, take the pole off first and then drop the spinnaker on the foredeck to windward of the forestay.

mark has to be left to leeward.

Trimming with the pole off

Trimming with the pole off is essentially the same as trimming with it on, except that the guy may have to be trimmed in (aft) to compensate for the distance the tack will move inboard when the pole is taken away. Obviously, this technique can only be used when running: if used when reaching, the spinnaker tack heads for the masthead as soon as it is released from the pole (bad news for those who like life on an even keel).

Float drop in light weather, no gybe

Simply remove the pole by tripping it away from the guy, taking it off the mast and stowing it. On boats with small spinnakers this is a one-person operation; on bigger boats it needs the foredeck hand to trip the pole, plus someone to tend the topping lift. As when gybing, make sure the lazy sheet is over the end of the pole before tripping, or the pole cannot fall away free when the topping lift is eased. The sail can either be brought down to windward or to leeward.

Float drop and gybe

Now we are becoming quite ambitious, although this method is much less complicated to do than to describe. It is also impressive to watch - but more important, it pays big dividends in time saved at the mark. It is used when approaching the mark on a run with the mark to be left to leeward, involving a gybe round the mark. Simply, the pole is taken off and stowed, the spinnaker allowed to float free, the yacht gybed and the spinnaker handed on to the foredeck on what is the weather side after the gybe.

Take the pole off and stow it. Gybe the main and the genoa: the foredeck hand will have to help the genoa across, and the genoa sheet hand must sheet it in to get it out of the way and ready for rounding up round the mark, which should now be mere feet away. The foredeck hand grabs what is now the lazy sheet (i.e. the slack rope to the spinnaker on the new weather side) and hauls it in, pulling the tack of the sail down to the deck at the mast and collapsing the sail from the luff. The sheet and lazy guy are let run completely to dump the spinnaker, which briefly flags out ahead of the forestay as the foot is gathered. At the same time, the halyard is thrown off the winch to let the sail fall onto the foredeck. The yacht is meanwhile rounding the mark hardening up, and so the spinnaker is blown into the weather side of the genoa which acts as a keep net, allowing the sail to come down onto the foredeck without going into the water.

THE TRIP

Before we leave spinnakers, let us recall the older method, still a good, safe way and probably the better to be used with a cobbled-together crew. It may be the safer if slightly slower way with a masthead spinnaker if the crew boss wants to be conservative. It can also be the method to use in a breeze below about ten knots, when there is not enough air to keep the spinnaker flowing horizontal.

The trip explained

The spinnaker pole is let forward until the tack is within reach; the clip between the guy and the tack is tripped (released) and the spinnaker flutters out like a flag behind the mainsail, held by the halyard and the sheet; the sheet is hauled in to reach the clew; the foot of the sail is gathered in so the sail resembles a long ribbon; the sail is lowered on the halyard and bundled down through the main hatch.

Trip technique

Set the new headsail. Leave it unsheeted (to keep the airflow into the spinnaker uninterrupted) until you are ready to take down the spinnaker, then trim it on the sheet (even if it will not set properly, have the sheet trimmed in but not over-trimmed; a flapping headsail now will merely get in the way of handing the spinnaker). Ease the pole forward so that the foredeck hand can reach the pole end and the trip line to the spinnaker clip on the guy. The foredeck hand may have to climb up in the pulpit if the pole has been carried high - on a medium-air run for example - or it may be necessary to lower the pole end on the topping lift.

The foredeck hand trips the sail by releasing the clip - most types work with a trip line. On bigger yachts, the clip may be of the type with a trigger: use a hardwood or metal spike to release the clip, not your finger.

Golden Rule: Mind your Head. Even on a small yacht, the load on the spinnaker guy can be enough to cause the pole to whip back aft as the sail is released, cracking the skull or splitting open the eyebrow of anyone foolish enough to have their head in the way. Similarly, the corner of the sail can flick with the viciousness of a whip as it flies free, so keep head and face below the pole as the sail is released.

As the sail flags out behind the mainsail, haul in the sheet to grab the clew and gather the foot, pulling in along the foot tape (usually white) until both corners of the sail are to hand. Let go the halyard, pulling the falling sail inboard under the boom and bundling it as quickly as possible down the hatch and out of the way.

Using this method it is important to have the spinnaker down before the yacht turns the mark. If you do not, and the yacht comes on the wind, the air flow carries the spinnaker out from under the lee of the main where it flags behind. You then have one, two, three or four people being pulled along the lee deck by the revitalised

Immediately the spinnaker is safely down, the foredeck hand clears up his domain, locking off the pole, securing the sheets and guys, and retrieving the bag if it is still up there.

spinnaker, now full of air and wilful life. This is at best very undignified. In the most brutal end-game of this unequal struggle, you can't hold the foot of the sail and must let go - and the yacht proceeds upwind with the spinnaker flying from the masthead like a giant burgee. (If this happens, the way to get the spinnaker back quickly is bite the bullet: turn the boat straight downwind so the spinnaker blows back either onto the mainsail or back into the lee of the mainsail, where it can be reached from on deck.)

CLEARING UP

Once the spinnaker is down and out of the way, there are several chores which must be done instantly, if not sooner.

- Unclip the halyard, the sheets and guys. The halyard should be stowed back on the mast, making sure that the lead from the halyard sheave at the top of the mast to the stowage clip is fair and the halyard has not caught around anything, like the upper spreader.
- Put the sheets and guys back on their stowage hooks up forward. Do not put them on opposite hooks - put them on the same hook, with one set led around the forestay. That way, time will be saved when next the spinnaker is needed: if they are on the wrong side when the next hoist comes, it is a simple matter to clip them together and haul them round. On smaller boats, you can leave them clipped together ready to be hauled round to the other side if necessary for the next spinnaker set without having to send anyone into the bow - but then make sure they are secured at the cockpit end.
- Secure the pole in its stowage, stow the topping lift back on the mast. Haul taut the foreguy, to help secure the forward end of the pole.
- Set up the babystay, if fitted.

Ready to tack?

As quickly as possible, ensure that the yacht is clear to tack. In particular this means checking the weather genoa sheet, to make sure it has not been trapped under the pole, or left inside the babystay when that was clipped back on. If the genoa now up is not the one that came down when the spinnaker was set, check that the sheet lead position on the weather side is correct. Do not forget to tell The Management: "Ready to tack".

PACKING THE SPINNAKER

Always re-pack the spinnaker as soon as it comes off: never leave it. A sudden windshift, the discovery by the navigator that you've just rounded the wrong mark, or anything else might conspire to mean that it will be needed again without warning.

Turtle pack

Most spinnakers are now set flying (ie loose, not in stops) from a specially shaped bag called a turtle. The turtle has an especially wide mouth, probably with the edges stiffened by a wire hoop, and a fabric top which closes over the mouth like a lid. Some have three flaps, kept closed by Velcro, but the purpose of all is to keep the sail close-bagged until the moment the halyard is hauled. A spinnaker can be packed by one person, but a big sail is best done either by two people or one person with four arms. Always start with the head.

1. Hook up the head. Most serious racing yachts have a hook or two on a bulkhead below, or the stump end of a deckhead grab handle might be used.
2. From the head, follow down each of the luff tapes towards the clews, pulling the twists out of the sail until the clew comes to hand.
3. Hook up each clew.
4. Follow along the foot tape, to make doubly sure that there are no twists in the sail.
5. From the head, gather up each luff tape between fingers and thumb until the whole

sail is hanging with the corners and edges uppermost, the bunt of the sail in a pile below.
6. Start pushing the sail into the turtle, from the middle of the bunt and working first towards the foot, then back towards the head, leaving the tapes and corners to last.
7. Pack the foot tape, leaving the two clews hanging over the edge of the turtle, then pack the top of the sail.
8. Fold the three corners into the turtle to lie on top of the packed sail, the head with the clews.
9. Clip or tie the three corners together using the top spring hook of the turtle, or the drawstring. This stops the corners becoming lost in the rest of the sail. Some turtles have lids designed to allow the three corners to protrude, held secure by a Velcro fastening.

Setting in stops

Large spinnakers, or those which will be set in heavy weather, are sometimes set in stops. These are simply ties of wool or light cotton, or most usually light elastic bands, tied around the sail every few feet to prevent it filling on its way to the masthead. The sail is fully hoisted in its stops, looking like a long sausage or loosely woven nylon rope. When it is up and out at the pole end, the sheet is hauled to pull the clews apart. The sail fills from the bottom upwards, opening like a huge flower as the stops break. You will need a large plastic bucket with the bottom cut out, and plentiful supply of elastic bands.

1. Fit a couple of dozen elastic bands over the outside of the bottom-less bucket.
2. Hook up the head, and follow through the luff tapes to untwist the sail, as if packing in the normal way.

3. Pass the spinnaker, head first and with the luff tapes together, through the bucket, slipping the elastic bands over the sail at intervals of two feet (0.5m) or so.

4. With the sail stopped, coil it into the turtle from the foot, but leaveng the foot itself (with clews stopped together) over the edge of the turtle so that sheet and guy can be clipped on.

WHEN TO USE WHAT

In reverse order of difficulty, here is a guide:

Mark to windward

Leeward drop. Any time except very light airs, when it upsets the genoa trim too much.
Leeward foredeck drop. Big boats with forehatches.
Windward foredeck drop. If approaching on a run in medium or light airs, when there is a forehatch.
Cockpit drop. Any time.

Mark to leeward

Float drop and gybe. Any time except heavy weather.
Cockpit drop. Any time, but early. Do not forget to lower the forward end of the pole to let the genoa gybe.

TRUE STORY

Golden Rule: Safest is usually quickest.
A 51-footer (15m) is running fast towards the downwind mark; she has a good lead and the crew are enjoying themselves, working well together and being very slick. A straight cockpit drop is called, but before the foot of the sail is properly inboard, the halyard is flung off. The top of the sail goes in the water with the yacht still doing nine knots; it fills; it starts dragging the rest of the sail in. Two men are pulled off their feet before they can let go; a third, caught up by the sail, is flicked up, out and overboard like a rag doll. The spinnaker, now a water-filled drogue, slews the boat around into a crash gybe; only prompt action by the man on the runner saves the mast, but the boom, slamming across the deck like a barn door in a gale, catches the mainsheet trimmer across the shoulders and topples him, breathless, over the guardrails into the water on the opposite side to the first man overboard.

Both men were recovered, indignant but otherwise unhurt, and even the spinnaker was retrieved at only the cost of a cut halyard, but it was a very subdued crew who took the boat up the final beat and back to her berth. They did not win. Slower is usually safer.

12   Around the Course

So far, we have broken crewing down into a series of basic jobs: setting the spinnaker, changing the headsail, loading a winch. These are the chores of crewing, the basic skills which have to be learned before we become working members of the team. Just as you have to learn to beat eggs before you can make a cake, so you have to learn to pack a spinnaker before you can take on a yacht race. Beaten eggs and packed spinnakers are not especially meritorious examples of human achievement when viewed in isolation: they are merely small parts of a greater whole. Seldom in a yacht race do we do one job and then go back to bed. One job flows into the next: we change the headsail, then trim it, then tack the yacht and so on. And throughout, sail trimming is a continuing preoccupation.

So all these skills are combined to sail the yacht round the course, and there should be no job on board which, when the need arises for it, fills the crew with horror and the thought 'Can't do that yet, haven't learned how to!'.

DIARY OF A RACE
Eight o'clock on race day

Eight o'clock on race day and the crew are assembling on the pontoon, while around them in the marina other crews are arriving and other yachts are making ready. The boat is opened up and bags are chucked on board, feet cleaned and the crew climb on board, the engine is started, the berthing lines let go and the yacht slides stern first out of her berth, her owner or sailing master at the helm, and turns her head towards the mouth of the river and the day's racing.

Usually, marinas being what they are, the first job is to rig all the movable gear that was stowed in safety below at the end of the previous outing. The strop, the lead blocks and the snatch blocks come up and are rigged or stowed in their appropriate places. The bowman climbs into his harness. The navigator has the details of the course and the weather forecast, and the latter is checked against the day to see if it bears any relation to reality. To give the forecasters their due, they are correct more often than not.

As the yacht motors to the start, the main cover comes off, the sail goes up and the first genoa of the day is prepared. On the way to the start is the time to talk any new crew member round the boat or, with several new members, time should have been made for at least a spinnaker gybe to let everyone find their place.

Arriving with plenty of time - an hour is not at all too much, and half-an-hour is the minimum - the yacht is taken up the first beat for fifteen minutes to try the headsail and let the navigator ponder the frequency of the wind oscillations. Back to the line and this is checked to find the bias. Maybe now we drop the headsail on deck and look at the others still sailing, sussing-out where we want to start.

Clear wind and speed are vital in the moments just after the start. The crew must provide the helmsman with the fastest boat in the fleet by trimming for power.

Ten minutes to go

Ten minutes to go, and the headsail goes back up, the engine left running but out of gear in case it is needed for a last-minute dash to the other end of the line. The sailing beforehand has let the newcomers settle in and everyone knows what they are supposed to be doing. Sheets port and starboard, grinding and tailing; someone on the runners; someone up in the pulpit to watch for opposite-tack yachts (in particular, starboard-tack yachts); someone at the mast, to help the genoa round in the tacks. The navigator is by the helmsman, calling the time to the start, watching for signals from the committee vessel.

Two minutes to go

"Two minutes to go... ease the genoa... ease the main... coming up, coming up... how far from the line?"
"Fifty yards."
"One-thirty to go," says the navigator.
"OK - power on the main, bring in the genoa, bearing away..."

"One minute."
"• • • • •! Too early... dump the main... luffing... right, bearing away again..."
"Thirty seconds."
"Trim the main, trim the genoa... going for it. Don't oversheet the genoa, I want speed."
"Fifteen seconds - seen the boat to leeward?"
"Yes - we'll roll over him."
"Five, four, three, two, one, gun. Second gun - recall - don't think it was us."
"We're OK," calls the bowman. "A good half-a-length off it; 2468 and 700 were over. 2468's turning back."

The race is under way

And so the race is under way, with our yacht tolerably well away, but too close to that boat to leeward. There is space to tack, so we do.

Now we are on port, crossing most of them: a bigger boat which started further up the line crosses ahead and a yellow boat, smoking along on starboard, looks set to cut us in half.

"Ready about - make it a good one...

Ready? Go!"

Our yacht slides neatly into and through her tack: on the yellow boat, close up on the weather quarter, the genoa backfills slightly and the helmsman bears away to the apparent header. Her crew are lined along the weather rail - hear no evil, speak no evil and see nothing at all - and it is only when she has to bear away even more for another `header' that her helmsman sees our bow emerge from behind his forestay.

"Quick, tack!" he yells and shoves the helm down. The crew scramble across the deck, the genoa catches briefly aback and the yacht stumbles round on to the other tack, her speed tumbling from six knots plus to one-and-a-half.

Clear air

Clear air now, and we can settle down for some fast sailing. The helmsman, no longer intent on squeezing up on the yacht to weather, eases off a fraction.

"Coming off a bit... there..On... on... on..."

As he calls his course, the genoa trimmer eases the sheet to keep the telltales streaming, the main trimmer lets the traveller a fraction down the track.

"Up point one... speed up point two... steady at six point nine" reports the navigator.

Throughout the race, trimmer and helmsman keep up a constant conversation, so that the response to changes in the wind strength and direction are co-ordinated. Others play their part in this segment of the race: the navigator monitors the course made good and the true strength and direction of the wind, either by calculation or by direct observation, using electronic instruments and performance computer.

"Headed another five - that's ten degrees since we tacked. I think we should go back - this won't be the paying tack any more."

"But I want to be over on this side of the course - there's less stream and I don't want to get too far away from *Puppeteer* and *Bandit*."

"OK, hold on - but if it breaks any more we have to go."

Up on the rail, there is more to do than simply make sure everyone's boots match: with helmsman and trimmers concentrating on speed, the crew play their part in watching for the darkening of the water which indicates a gust.

"Pressure in twenty... fifteen... ten... here it is."

The yacht heels more; and the genoa luff lifts as the puff also slightly heads.

"Main going down," as the mainsheet is eased down the traveller.

"Sheet coming in."

"Bearing away."

"Sheet going out."

"Coming back up" - and the interplay goes on.

Rounding the first mark

Unlike dinghy races, only a minority of races for yachts are sailed on perfect Olympic courses. Most courses use natural obstacles or existing navigation marks as turning points.

Smart work with the nav computer shows that the next leg will be a shy reach, too shy for the spinnaker, so the jib-top comes up on deck. The genoa is up on the wire halyard, in the port groove, so with the yacht on starboard tack the foredeck crew quickly flake the reacher along the starboard rail, hook on the tack and feed the head into the starboard feeder, then put a couple of sail ties round both sail and guardrail. The starboard spinnaker halyard is buttoned on to the head of the jib-top, the slack taken up and the halyard secured, tensioned lightly against the sail tie so there is no danger of the loose halyard swinging out round a spreader end. The yacht tacks for the mark, and now the sail is in the right place, to leeward of the genoa but already bent on and ready to hoist.

On that yellow boat the crew have left the preparations too late. Although she too has tacked for the mark, two of them are still sliding around the foredeck, getting their feet wet and upsetting the genoa while they try to bundle the jib-top under the skirt of the genoa and feed the head into the starboard groove which is now to leeward and outside the genoa. If they are not careful, the foaming bow wave will catch the unattached sail and wash it aft, to trail like a drogue from out between the stanchions. There it goes...

Getting ready for the next reach

Well round the first mark now, but it is only a short port-tack reach to the next mark which also has to be left to starboard: from there it is going to be a broad reach on starboard, so that means a gybe-set at the coming mark.

The 20/30 is brought on deck and taken to the rail, port side. In the cockpit, the sheets and guys are taken off their stowage cleats, and up forward are clipped to the sail. Happily, the foredeck hand had clipped both sets to the same stowage eye, even more happily to the port stowage eye, so there is no need to sit in the pulpit or struggle the lines round the front of the reacher. The port spinnaker halyard is brought to the rail by the sail, and clipped there - not yet to the sail in case, untended,

its weight pulls the head of the sail out of the bag.

Now the pole is unshipped from its stowage along the starboard side of the foredeck. The starboard-side guy is put through the pole end and the topping lift clipped on, the forward end of the pole pushed to leeward of the tack of the jib-top and into the pulpit and then the aft end lifted and fitted into the mast cup. A final check on all the leads, and the halyard is clipped on.

The yacht rushes towards the mark. The helmsman bears away round the mark... the main trimmer hauls on the sheet, the boom comes to the centreline, gybes and the traveller crashes across the track - the (expletive deleted) traveller car should have been centred, and wasn't. Fortunately, no one's hand was in the way.

The jib-top sheet is eased and taken on the other side, on the secondary winch. On the starboard side it is thrown right off the winch and the spinnaker guy swiftly loaded on while the foredeck hand lifts the end of the pole. In the cockpit the mainsheet hand, sheet cleated, overhauls the slack on the topping lift as the winch rings, and with the weight of the pole held by the topping lift, drops the line into the cam cleat. The foredeck hand runs to the mast and flings himself on the halyard. "Wrong one, Brian - it's on the port halyard. Twit!'

The correct halyard is hauled hand over hand while at the winch the tailer overhauls the slack. Simultaneously in the cockpit the guy is being hauled aft on its winch and two turns of the spinnaker sheet have been thrown on to the port primary, but plenty of slack left. The spinnaker blossoms out, the pole swinging aft and the sail flagging briefly while another turn is thrown on to the halyard winch and the handle fitted so the last eighteen inches of halyard can be wound up.

The spinnaker sheet is trimmed while the halyard winch hand, having secured the spinnaker halyard, moves to the reacher halyard and lets it go as the foredeck hand, moving forward again from the mast, catches the sail and hands it down onto the deck. The helmsman settles on the course which the navigator had whispered in his ear just as they approached the mark, and the trimmers set about settling the sail down. Pole aft, ease the sheet, up on the topping lift...raise the inboard end of the pole...take up the slack on the foreguy...

On the yellow boat, the gybe set is a trifle hurried, the sail going up before the guy was loaded on the winch properly. The pole is slow coming back, the spinnaker half fills behind the reacher, swings once, twice... Oh dear. They've hour-glassed it.

Changing the spinnaker

The wind has gradually lightened and drawn aft, and this is now definitely the wrong sail: we should be using the half-ounce. Time for a peel. With the 20/30 up on the port halyard, we must use the starboard halyard for the half-ounce, and this gives us an inside hoist/outside drop. That's handy.

The sail is brought up, and the clip on the bottom of the turtle hooked to the eye at the base of the aft, leeward leg of the pulpit. The lazy guy is transferred direct to the clew of the existing spinnaker. The sheet trimmer loads the lazy guy onto the secondary winch and transfers the weight of the sail to it, throwing the now slack sheet off the winch: the foredeck hand, moving to the lee shrouds, grabs the slack bight of the sheet and walks it forward until, briefly hauling the clew of the sail inboard by

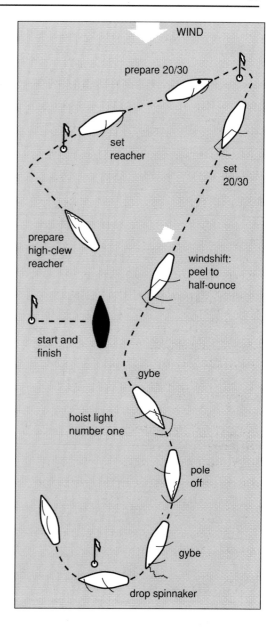

hand, he reaches up and trips the sheet clip from the sail. He clips the sheet to the clew of the new spinnaker, checking to see the lead is outside everything.

He unclips the starboard spinnaker halyard from its stowage, puts the climbing hook of his harness through the hard eye, and spins the lock closed. In the cockpit, the lazy sheet is loaded on to the secondary winch (the guy is on the primary) and the weight transferred, slackening the guy so it can be thrown off. The tail of the starboard spinnaker halyard is out on the winch, and with a winder and a tailer the bowman is hauled swiftly up to grab the spinnaker pole and pull himself out to the end. He unclips the slackened guy and pulls it through the beak of the pole, swinging inboard again at the same time. With precision timing the halyard is eased to deposit him gently on deck.

Unclipping the starboard spinnaker halyard from his harness he leads it forward and round the forestay, back to the sail where he clips it on. He clips the guy to the tack of the sail, and signals all is ready. Up goes the halyard as the guy comes aft and the sheet is trimmed and the new sail sets, somewhat imperfectly, inside the 20/30. The port halyard is tensioned on the winch, the button on the stopper lever pressed and the lever flicked up and off. The sheet of the old sail is hauled in fast as the port halyard is first surged then flung off the winch. The foredeck hand grabs the old sheet, gathers the 20/30 hand-over-hand as it falls slowly and gracefully down the outside of the swelling half-ounce and the guy is let run. The 20/30 is spirited away.

Gybe and gybe again

It all goes so smoothly that on the yellow boat, now a little way astern, they don't even notice that we have peeled. Our speed, which had been dropping each time our 20/30 dropped, steadies and then, as the lighter and fuller half-ounce continues to float high and free above us, slowly creeps back up. The wind continues to veer until, not far short of the mark, we have to slip in a gybe - smooth enough, but

now we will have to gybe again as we round the mark for the beat back home.

The jib-top is cleared up from where we dumped it and packed away, and the light number one comes up to take its place. With only a little way to go to the mark, we prepare it on the port side, where we'll need it after the gybe back, rather than on the starboard side where it properly should go. Up it goes, on the central, wire genoa halyard but with the clew taken right forward so that it does not interfere with the still-flying spinnaker. The sheets are left with plenty of slack.

Coming into the mark, off comes the pole while the spinnaker looks after itself, floating high and setting even better while square running like this without the overshort pole the measurement rule requires us to use. With the pole stowed, the yacht begins her gybe, only a length or two short of the mark now. As the main boom crosses the centreline and the genoa trimmer brings home the genoa sheet, the foredeck hand, with a back-up, grabs the spinnaker sheet and hauls the clew of the sail swiftly down to the deck. The starboard guy is let run and the two on the foredeck swiftly pull the foot of the sail round the forestay even as the yacht turns the mark. The halyard is let go, and as the yacht hardens up round the mark the sail flutters neatly down onto the foredeck and is bundled down the forehatch.

On that yellow boat, when they eventually reach the mark, they will probably take the spinnaker off before gybing, and take even longer to complete the last length or two into the mark in the failing afternoon breeze. Meanwhile, our own yacht settles down for the final beat home, watching the windshifts and the telltales...

13　Life on board

As soon as you arrive on board, find out where you can stow your gear. You will most probably be given a locker of your own, and it should be a point of pride with you that all your gear - boots and oilskins, which have their own stowage, excepted - is either in there or on you. Your watch and sunglasses, contact lens case and personalised sweatband will not please the navigator when they turn up on the chart table. (Locker, nowadays, is a quaint term left over from more elegant times. What we are probably talking about is an open-topped sailcloth pouch hanging on a bulkhead.)

WHAT TO TAKE

How much you take depends on how big the boat is and how long the race is going to be. Aim to take with you as little as possible, but at the same time do not go without something you need. The crew member who turns up with just boots and one light bag is always welcome, but the person who has to keep borrowing sweaters, towels and someone else's oilskin is just a nuisance. The crew member who gets wet and cold in the first two hours because he or she has not brought the proper clothing is a liability.

Some skippers may well tell you exactly what to bring, and exactly what you will be provided with on board: others may say "Whatever you like, as long as it's only in one bag" while the fanatical may give you a maximum weight of gear you can bring.

Always take
- Oilskins
- Boots
- The clothes you stand up in, plus one layer (it is always colder on the water than on the land).

For more than a day race, add
- A change of clothes, from the skin out.
- Two towels, one big one, and one for round the neck.
- Enough personal hygiene equipment to make your proximity bearable by those around you (it can be truly awful sharing the rail with someone who hasn't brushed their teeth for four days).
- Shore-going clothes, if needed.

You should check
- Whether bedding is provided, or whether you bring your own sleeping bag.
- Whether safety harnesses are provided, or whether you bring your own (and then bring your own anyway).
- Whether you should bring shore-going clothes, and if so the standard of dress expected. Although many yacht clubs are informal, the owner may not wish his boat to be represented ashore by a bunch of ruffians who look as if they own only one pair of jeans each, none less than eight years old. In addition, the owner and other crew members may want to eat ashore in a good restaurant or a more formal club: for

many of us, offshore racing is a social as well as a sporting pastime, and you don't want to miss the party just because you are the only one who did not bring a tie.

Dressed to sail

A T-shirt and a pair of jeans, sweaters added according to environment, is still basic working wear for most offshore sailors, and is entirely adequate for the occasional crew. Several manufacturers however now produce specialised clothing, usually as part of an integrated system with a trade name like Warm Wear or Polar Wear, which crew who sail a lot find it worthwhile to buy.

A typical complete outfit might thus consist of long-sleeved undervest, with long-legged pants, worn next the skin but over personal underwear; a lightweight roll-neck sweater; a sleeveless, long-legged quilted garment; a quilted jacket. On top of this is worn oilskin trousers and jacket, with thick warm socks on the feet and boots.

This outfit is very warm - too warm for an inshore race on a sunny day - but the system is designed so that bits such as the long underwear can be left off when necessary. The advantage of such an outfit is its comfort and suitability - it is designed after all for offshore sailing - coupled with lightness and lack of bulk. Wearing such an outfit, only three layers are required and the modern materials of which this thermal clothing is made are very light and are thus easy to stow and carry.

One disadvantage is that it is a curious-looking outfit in which to walk up the High Street of the town that the race visits, and will draw even more curious glances on the train coming home after the race

(especially a three-day race); so normal shoreside clothes, albeit jeans and sweater, must be taken as well, unless the boat is going out only to race.

Oilskins

For day sailing, a simple anorak and waterproof trousers will usually be enough to keep out the worst of the wet, but for longer races or sailing at night, something more substantial is needed. A good suit of offshore oilskins has:

- Chest-high trousers, combined with a zip-up jacket.
- A jacket and trousers that are lined, loosely, with a lightweight waterproof material that cuts down condensation inside the suit, and adds a measure of thermal insulation.
- All the seams of both garments welded or glued and taped, to keep them waterproof.
- Cuffs on trousers and jacket with some sort of seal, for when it is really wet.
- Jacket with some sort of integral buoyancy, even if it's only a lining of closed-cell foam.
- A jacket with a high, stand-up collar which will protect the ears, with a tuck-away hood for when it is raining or really cold.
- A safety harness built in to the jacket, probably with closable pockets to stow the buckles when not in use.
- A whistle on a lanyard stitched into one jacket pocket, for use as an emergency locator if you go overboard.

Additional features might include an inflatable collar, possibly with a small gas bottle; light-reflecting tape on the front, at the wrists (to be seen when waving) and on the back of the collar, to help find you in the dark if you go overboard; `hand-warmer' pockets under the main pockets; two-way zips to allow you to get into certain areas of the suit without doing a mid-ocean strip act. If you intend sailing more than once or twice a season, one of these suits is a worthwhile investment.

Drysuits

Offshore yachts are wet. Offshore crews spend much time on deck, often spending hours just sitting on the rail. Drysuit tops and even full drysuits are often worn, especially by foredeck crews who work at · the wettest end of the yacht. Their disadvantage is that they can be devilish hot to work in, and despite attempts by various manufacturers over many years, the drysuit which does not produce quantities of internal condensation has yet to be invented. The condensation problem can be partly overcome by wearing quilted or piled so-called 'wicking' clothing underneath the drysuit.

Footwear

High-grip footwear is essential. For long (more than a few hours) races in cold (European or North American) water boots rather than deck-shoes are recommended. Go for a pair with extra thick soles which will act as thermal insulation between you and the hard, cold deck.

SAFETY

While the first edition of this book was in preparation, one of Britain's best-known and respected racing seamen lost his life through falling overboard two miles from harbour on a routine delivery voyage. It was a salutary reminder to everyone that accidents do happen and that safety systems can fail. Since then, regular man-overboard incidents have continued to occur, mercifully few being fatal.

Non-sailors place much emphasis on the wearing of lifejackets while afloat, but it is worth remembering that a lifejacket is utterly useless, save as a pillow, on a yacht. Off the yacht, it's worth increases dramatically, but it is always much better to stay on the yacht in the first place.

Harnesses

There should be a safety harness on board for every crew member, and before each race each crew member - the newcomer especially - should find his or her safety harness, put it on and adjust the fit: not so tight that it restricts breathing, but tight enough to hold the wearer securely. Put the harness on and then imagine yourself going over the side, with only the tether between you and your death. Is the chest strap so loose that as soon as the tether jerks taut, inevitably from a point above your head, the buckle is jerked upwards and hits you in the teeth? Rendered thus unconscious, your arms hanging limp, will the harness just pull off over your head? For this reason, most serious crew have their own harness, clearly marked with their name and adjusted to fit. Best of all, perhaps, is a harness built into your jacket - but there are times, in warm weather at night for example, when you might want a harness but not the jacket.

Safety stowage

When you get on board, acquaint yourself with the location of all the boat's emergency equipment, from flares and the liferaft to tools, including things like the bolt croppers. Safety is not just about emergency. Knowing just where you can grab a sharp knife (there should be one stowed at the mast, for example) can easily save a developing snarl-up, or more seriously save a fellow crewman from injury - even losing a finger or worse. If the mast goes over the side, quick and efficient crew work replacing the headless chicken syndrome can easily limit the damage, while too much headless chicken work can leave the mast over the side and puncturing a hole in the hull.

A well-organised boat should have a clearly posted stowage plan, like the sail stowage plan we spoke of in Chapter 3. You should be confident you can find all the tools in the dark, when it is wet and cold and blowing hard. That is when you are most likely to need them.

SEASICKNESS

Seasickness affects, to a greater or lesser degree, nearly all those who race offshore, and it particularly affects the inexperienced. Do not be afraid to bring your own favourite remedy with you, or to find out what other people take. There is only one infallible cure for seasickness: sit under an apple tree for half-an-hour. In addition, some simple precautions will reduce the chances of being sick:

- Take no alcohol for at least 24 hours before the race.
- Avoid greasy or exotic foods for at least 24 hours before the race.
- Get a good night's sleep before the race.
- Do not let yourself get cold and wet on the race.

WATCH SYSTEMS

Traditionally, the crew of a sailing vessel is divided into sections called watches, each in the charge of a mate and each coming on duty at set times of the day. The usual length of a watch at sea is four hours, and in the British naval system two two-hour watches (the Dog Watches) in the afternoon ensure a rotation so that all watches take an equal share of night and day, light and darkness. This system, so admirable for running a vessel with a regular routine and a long voyage ahead of her, has proven to be one of the least efficient ways of running a racing yacht, but the traditions of the sea die hard and many yachts, especially those with `old and bold' owners, stick to it.

The rolling watch

If two watches are to be used, three hours is plenty long enough at night for a nine-to-five human fresh - or rather jaded - from a week in the office, while few races are long enough to let the crew settle comfortably into a proper watch routine. Most successful boats use a rolling watch system, where each member of the crew goes off or comes on at a different time to all the others, while if the crew is large enough (six or more) the skipper and the navigator do not take regular watches, but are on call, if not on deck, all the time.

In a six-person crew, it works like this: 1 and 2 are skipper and navigator, and outside the watch routine. They arrange between themselves to cover for each other when one is below. The remaining crew - 3,4,5 and 6 - have a basic watch of two hours on deck, one hour sheltering below but on immediate call which means fully clad but cat-napping, and one hour off watch, sleeping.

So we start the race with all crew on deck having a great time racing the boat. As night comes on, but before exhaustion from the hard day at the office overtakes everyone, we start the watches. Crew members 3 and 6 stay on watch, and 4 and 5 go below with 5 remaining on call. An hour later 4 comes back on, 6 goes on call and 5 stays below for an hour's more kip. An hour later 3 goes on call, 5 comes up and 6 goes off. An hour later, 6 comes back on deck and 5 goes below on call, and so on.

In this example it is assumed that everyone is equally good at all tasks, including steering, and that either the navigator or skipper is always up and about. One hour may not sound much for sleep, but with the system running it is really two hours (with perhaps an interruption in the first), and this is adequate over a short race. Over longer races skipper and navigator would have to come into the rota to give longer breaks, or with more people on board longer breaks would occur naturally.

The advantage of the rolling system is that it avoids that awful hour when those on deck are watching the clock instead of the sails, and it avoids the break in continuity that occurs when there is a complete crew change at the change of watch. With the rolling system there is always someone fresh in their first hour on deck, and yet someone who has been on deck long enough to keep track of what is going on outside the guardrails.

BEING ASKED BACK

Racing regularly on big boats is a very satisfying hobby, and becoming a reliable and valuable crew member is the easiest way for most of us to enjoy this hobby: owning big boats is an expensive pastime, and for most of us owning and campaigning a racing boat of over 33ft (10m) is just a dream.

The very big boats, and the top racing boats, are in the main crewed by young men who are professionals: either full-time racing sailors, or employed by sailmakers,

sparmakers or others in the business - or occasionally in one of the owner's companies. They race boats as part and parcel of their job, and to compete for places with these full-time experts the true amateur has to be very good, very dedicated and have plenty of free time. This, however, is only the highly visible tip of the offshore racing iceberg. Most yachts outside the handful of true international racers are crewed by amateurs: once into the racing scene and tolerably competent, good crews should have no trouble finding a boat which is good fun to race on, where the lifestyle afloat and ashore suits their taste and pocket and where they can become a member of a happy team.

Who pays?

There are as many ways of running a boat as there are owners, and it is impossible to give hard and fast rules about who pays for what or who does what. On larger boats, especially those at the sharp end of the racing, it is normal for the owner to pay for just about everything, perhaps even providing oilskins and some clothing for the regular crew, especially if 'team colours' are worn. On such yachts food and drink (serious boats are alcohol-free zones, but the crew make up for it ashore) are normally provided, but it is reasonable on boats on a less lavish budget for the crew to pay a share of the direct costs - food, drink, entry fees - of the race. Many smaller yachts run on a co-operative basis, where the regular crew pay a contribution to the yacht's upkeep, but for this they have in return a greater say in the yacht's programme and may have the use of the boat at times when she is not racing.

ENJOY YOURSELF!

Other yachting titles from Fernhurst Books of interest to the racing crewman

Boat Cuisine *by June Raper*
Boat Engines 3e *by Dick Hewitt*
Bottoms Up *by Robert Watson*
Celestial Navigation *by Tom Cunliffe*
Charter & Flotilla Handbook *by Claire Wilson*
Children Afloat *by Pippa Driscoll*
Coastal & Offshore Navigation *by Tom Cunliffe*
Cruising Crew *by Malcolm McKeag*
Cruising Skipper *by John Mellor*
Electronics Afloat *by Tim Bartlett*
First Aid Afloat *by Dr. Robert Haworth*
Heavy Weather Cruising *by Tom Cunliffe*
Inshore Navigation *by Tom Cunliffe*
Knots & Splices *by Jeff Toghill*
Log Book for Cruising under Sail *by John Mellor*
Marine SSB Operation *by Michael Gale*
Marine VHF Operation *by Michael Gale*
Mental & Physical Fitness for Sailing *by Alan Beggs, John Derbyshire and Sir John Whitmore*
Navigation, Strategy & Tactics *by Stuart Quarrie*
Protests and Appeals *by Bryan Willis*
Racing Skipper *by Robin Aisher*
Ready About! *by Mike Peyton*
The Rules in Practice *by Bryan Willis*
Sail to Freedom *by Bill & June Raper*
Sailing: A Beginner's Manual *by John Driscoll*
Sailpower *by Lawrie Smith & Andrew Preece*
Sails *by John Heyes*
Simple Electronic Navigation *by Mik Chinery*
Simple GPS Navigation *by Mik Chinery*
Tactics 2e by Rodney Pattisson
Tuning Yachts and Small Keelboats *by Lawrie Smith*
Weather at Sea *by David Houghton*
Wind Strategy 2e *by David Houghton*

If you would like a free full-colour brochure please write, phone or fax us:

Fernhurst Books, Duke's Path, High Street, Arundel,
West Sussex BN18 9AJ, England

Telephone: 01903 882277   Fax: 01903 882715